The Essential Guide to MUSIC THEORY

Everything You Need to Learn the Basics and Beyond

JAMES ROSCHER

Copyright © 2023 by James Roscher | Musicora Publishing

All rights reserved. No part of this book may be reproduced or transmitted in any form or by any means, electronic or mechanical, including photocopying, recording, scanning, or otherwise, without the publisher's explicit permission in writing.

Limit of Liability/Disclaimer of Warranty: the publisher and the author make no representations or warranties with respect to the accuracy or completeness of the contents of this work and specifically disclaim all warranties, including without limitation warranties of fitness for a particular purpose. Although every precaution has been taken in the preparation of this book, the publisher and author assume no responsibility for errors or omissions. Neither is any liability assumed for damages resulting from the use of information contained herein.

The fact that an individual, organization or website is referred to in this work as a citation and/or potential source of further information does not mean that the author or the publisher endorses the information the individuals, organization or website may provide or recommendations they/it may make.

Musicora Publishing. The Essential Guide to Music Theory. Everything You Need to Learn the Basics and Beyond

Author: James Roscher
ISBN: 979-88-5685-406-9

Musicora Publishing
www.musicora.co
info@musicora.co

The wise musicians are those who play what they can master.
~ Duke Ellington ~

This book is dedicated to the masters that have come before and those still to come.

Table of Contents

Introduction 1
    Everyone Has Music Inside Them 1
    How to Use This Book 2
    What is Music Theory? 3
        The Basics 3
        How Do We Use Music Theory? 4
        How Do We Learn Music Theory? 5

1. Exploring Pitch 7
    What is Pitch? 7
        How Do We Describe Pitch? 7
        The Music Alphabet 9
    Reading Music Notation 10
        The Staff 11
        Clefs 11
    Practice Time! 18
        Chapter 1 Questions 18
        Chapter 1 Exercises 19
    Conclusion 20

2. Exploring Rhythm 23
    What is Rhythm? 23
    How is Rhythm Organized in Music? 24
    Exploring Notes 24
        What Are the Different Types of Notes? 24
        The Note Pyramid 26

Rests: How Silence is Marked in Music 27
How do Time Signatures Affect Notes? 28
Feel the Rhythm 30
Practice Time! 32
    Chapter 2 Questions 32
    Chapter 2 Exercises 33
Conclusion 34

3. Exploring Intervals 37

What is an Interval? 37
The Distance Between Notes 39
Intervals on the Music Staff 41
Melodic vs. Harmonic Intervals 44
Practice Time! 44
    Chapter 3 Questions 44
    Chapter 3 Exercises 45
Conclusion 45

4. Exploring Scales 47

Combine Pitches and Intervals to Build Scales 47
Using Intervals to Build the Major Scale 48
Using Intervals to Build the Minor Scale 51
    Natural Minor Scale 51
    Harmonic Minor Scale 53
    Melodic Minor Scale 54
Pentatonic, Chromatic and Whole Tone Scales 55
Scale Degrees 55
Understanding Relative Major and Relative Natural Minor 56
    Relative Minor 56
    Relative Major 57

Functional Words..59
Learning to Use Solfege..61
Practice Time 63
   Chapter 4 Questions..*63*
   Chapter 4 Exercises...*64*
Conclusion..65

5. Exploring Harmony through Building Chords 67
The Basics of Chords 67
Different Types of Chords 68
   Major Triads...*68*
   Minor Triads..*70*
   Diminished Triads..*72*
   Augmented Triads..*74*
Building a Chord Scale 76
Adding in Roman Numerals 77
Chord Progression 77
Chord Inversion 78
Practice Time! 79
   Chapter 5 Questions..*79*
   Chapter 5 Exercises...*80*
Conclusion..81

6. Key Signatures & Circle of Fifths..83
Key Signatures: How Pitches are Organized 83
Why Different Music Keys? 84
Where to Find the Key Signature? 85
The Circle of Fifths 87
The Major and Relative Minor Keys with Sharps (♯) 89
The Major and Relative Minor Keys with Flats (♭)........................90

    A Few Quick Tricks to Identify the Key Signature 92

    Practice Time! 94

        Chapter 6 Questions 94

        Chapter 6 Exercises 94

    Conclusion 95

7. Exploring the Modes 97

    What is a Mode? 97

        Why Bother Learning Modes? 100

    The Intervallic Patterns of Modes 100

        Ionian Mode 100

        Dorian Mode 101

        Phrygian Mode 102

        Lydian Mode 102

        Mixolydian Mode 103

        Aeolian Mode 104

        Locrian Mode 104

    The Modes on a Spectrum 105

    Tips to Create a Mode 105

    Practice Time! 106

        Chapter 7 Questions 106

        Chapter 7 Exercises 107

    Conclusion 108

8. Exploring Seventh Chords 109

    A Wider World of Harmony 109

    What are Seventh Chords? 109

    The Main Families of Seventh Chords 110

        Major Seventh Chords 110

        Dominant Seventh Chords 112

    Minor Seventh Chords..*113*

    Diminished Seventh Chords..*115*

  Building the Seventh Chord Scale...118

  Chord Extensions 120

    Major 9th *121*

    Major 7th ♯11 ....*121*

    Dominant 9th..**122**

    Dominant 13th *122*

    Minor 9th..**123**

  Practice Time!..123

    Chapter 8 Questions..*123*

    Chapter 8 Exercises...*124*

  Conclusion...125

9. Exploring Dynamics and Musical Markings............................. 127

  Dynamics: How Volume is Described in Music 127

  Linking Dynamics Together with Crescendo, Diminuendo,
    and the Slur 129

    Crescendo...*129*

    Diminuendo *130*

    Slur, Legato Mark, or Phrase Mark *131*

  Metronome Markings and Indications of Speed and Style.....................132

  Marking Octaves..133

  Marking Directives 135

  Practice Time!..136

    Chapter 9 Questions..*136*

    Chapter 9 Exercises...*136*

  Conclusion...137

Final Words: Music Theory is the Key 139
Glossary of Keywords 141
ANSWERS: Question & Exercise 149
   1. Exploring Pitch 149
      Questions 149
      Exercises 150
   2. Exploring Rhythm 151
      Questions 151
      Exercises 152
   3. Exploring Intervals 153
      Questions 153
      Exercises 154
   4. Exploring Scales 154
      Questions 154
      Exercises 156
   5. Exploring Harmony Through Building Chords 157
      Questions 157
      Exercises 158
   6. Key Signatures & Circle of Fifths 160
      Questions 160
      Exercises 161
   7. Exploring the Modes 161
      Questions 161
      Exercises 162
   8. Exploring Seventh Chords 163
      Questions 163
      Exercises 164

    9. Exploring Dynamics & Musical Markings 165
        Questions *165*
        Exercises *166*
About the Author **167**
About the Publisher **169**

Introduction

Have you ever thought, "I am not musical or rhythmical at all," or "I am too old to learn something new"? Have you ever started to learn an instrument on your own only to stop because you think to yourself, "I don't have enough time," "How do I know if I am doing things correctly?", or "I can't afford real music lessons"?

If so, you are not alone. Everyone struggles with thoughts like these from time to time. But don't fear. It is completely possible to overcome these roadblocks and develop your understanding of music theory, and confidence in your own musicality and creativity. Doubt is a natural phenomenon, and it is important to learn to transform and transcend it in your creative development.

Every single person has rhythm. If you are alive with a beating heart, you have rhythm. You experience rhythm every single day in many ways, including patterns of sleeping and waking, eating, and breathing. Think about how rhythm intersects with your life and how you already perceive rhythm. Do you notice when time seems to speed up or slow down? Do you ever find yourself snapping your fingers or tapping on the steering wheel while driving?

Everyone Has Music Inside Them

Music is just a way of organizing naturally occurring rhythmic patterns into a coherent, creative expression. Everyone has an innate musicality; however, only some are given the keys to access this musicality. You are never too old to learn new skills and develop new talents. In fact, many studies show the benefits of practicing instruments to keep the brain younger for longer, to create new neural pathways, and even as a potential antidote to memory loss.

Learning an instrument provides a creative outlet for stress and aids relaxation, helps develop self-confidence, and can be a fun way to engage with new friends. These friendships position you in the world of music and serve as inspiration to continue developing your skills and knowledge.

You do not need to spend hours every day practicing to develop proficiency and a functional understanding of music theory. The most important factor in your progress is maintaining a coherent, logical routine and sticking to it. Twenty or thirty minutes of focused and disciplined practice four or five days a week will yield faster results than a one-hour cram session one day per week.

Think of the musicians that inspire you. How do you think they reached the level of achievement you admire? They certainly did not just pick up the guitar and immediately become virtuosos. A disciplined and consistent work ethic and a desire to create fueled their success. Let this be your fuel as well.

How to Use This Book

This book is designed for the complete beginner who is interested in understanding music theory. By the end of the program, the student will have developed a solid understanding of many concepts. They will have gained knowledge of scales, chords and the ability to manipulate music theory tools. The student will explore note reading, how to use time and key signatures, the structure and formula of many scales and chords, the structure of chord progressions, the Circle of Fifths and its applications, as well as knowledge of common terms used in music.

The concepts in this book are presented in an easy-to-understand format, using simple language that anyone can grasp, regardless of their previous knowledge of music. Many examples, diagrams, and tests are provided to help ensure comprehension and functional understanding of the material. By no means is this all there ever is to learn but it is an excellent start!

Introduction

Music theory is commonly regarded as a high-minded and pretentious topic that is often scoffed at by many "self-taught" musicians. This book helps break down this barrier and reconstruct the narrative that learning about music theory will narrow your mindset, skills, and creativity.

The opposite is the truth. By following the programs in this book, you will develop a functional knowledge of music theory that will serve you in all your music-making endeavors and help to expand your perceptions of what is possible with music.

What is Music Theory?

In its most basic form, music theory is simply the study of the underlying patterns and tendencies in music. Music theory is in no way a hard and fast set of rules. Rather, think of it as a set of words and concepts to better understand the music you hear and enjoy and tools you can use to create interesting and beautiful sounds. Of course, you do not need to understand music theory to create beautiful and captivating music. But, understanding how you can use the tools of music theory in your creative work is undoubtedly advantageous.

The Basics

In general, music comprises three interconnected elements: pitch, rhythm, and harmony. Think of these elements as analogous to visual elements. Pitches combine to form melodies, like lines in a drawing or brush strokes in a painting. They give form and shape to music but, on their own, are one-dimensional.

Rhythms animate our world. We live in a dimension of time; everything moves, vibrates, and every piece of our reality has a propulsive beat that drives it forward. Rhythms are like the skeleton and muscles of music; they give it motion and drive it forward.

Harmonies are like colors and gradients, shadows and highlights. They imbue the music with depth and scope, deepening and defining melodies. Harmony can be powerful and intense, like ocean waves crashing against the cliffs, or calm and plaintive, like clouds floating over a sunlit field.

These three elements act in concert with one another to create music. Each area is capable of immense strength and can be explored deeply. In the following chapters, we will dive into these three elements and leave with a greater understanding of harmony, melody, and rhythm.

This book provides a firm foundation for understanding these concepts and encourages you to explore beyond and deeper into the fascinating word of music. As you embark on your musical journey, you will feel compelled to progress gradually, allowing your curiosity to drive you forward.

How Do We Use Music Theory?

Music theory is used in many interesting ways. We can use music theory to:

- Analyze music that has already been composed. By analyzing musical structures like chord progressions, melodic phrases, and rhythmic elements, we can identify patterns and tendencies that occur regularly in music. This helps us to build our knowledge base and understand the underlying features of music, which is both exciting and valuable.

- Describe and communicate musical concepts. Music theory gives us the tools and concepts to describe tendencies in music. If we understand the basic language of music theory, we can effectively communicate musical concepts in a straightforward and direct way that is easily understood by other musicians. For example, it is much easier to describe a chord progression as A minor - D minor - E major than to try and describe some shape on the guitar or piano or point with your fingers to certain notes.

- Help us create music. Of course, it is not necessary to understand music theory in order to compose music. Many musicians claim to know nothing of music theory yet are fabulous composers and songwriters.

However, just because somebody else claimed to find no use in it, does not mean you should avoid learning at least the basics of the subject.

By understanding the basic patterns and tendencies in music and learning to manipulate tools like musical keys, scales, rhythms, and chord progressions, you can build a unique and personal musical language and stretch the boundaries of what is possible for you in music. This is certainly a worthwhile endeavor.

How Do We Learn Music Theory?

Music theory is not terribly difficult to learn. Keep in mind that music theory is essentially just a set of tools used to explain tendencies and patterns in music and not a strict set of rules, and you will be fine. Try to avoid dogmatic viewpoints and practice slowly and consistently – you will come to understand how you can use music theory in no time!

In the following chapters, we will explore pitch, rhythm, and harmony in different contexts. We will provide a set of keywords for each chapter that you should memorize and try to understand. There will be many examples of concepts and small quizzes at the end of each chapter to test your skills and understanding. When you are ready, dive in!

James Roscher
Author

1

Exploring Pitch

Keywords: notes, music alphabet, octave, the staff, treble clef, bass clef, middle C, the grand staff

What is Pitch?

In music, the term "pitch" is used to identify the relative high or low sound of a note. Pitch is determined by the frequency of a sound vibration moving through space. Measured in hertz (Hz), high-frequency vibrations create higher pitches, and low-frequency vibrations create lower pitches. So, at its fundamental, pitch is sound; however, add elements of time, rhythm, and harmony, well then we have music. All music comprise various pitches combined to be pleasing to the ear.

How Do We Describe Pitch?

To express pitch, musicians use the **music alphabet**, as shown below:

$$A - A\sharp - B - C - C\sharp - D - D\sharp - E - F - F\sharp - G - G\sharp$$

The music alphabet with sharps ♯

The music alphabet is an essential tool for learning how to read and write music. It consists of **twelve alpha letters** that, when combined, can create a unique musical language. Each letter corresponds to a note value and the notes can be arranged into scales, chords, and melodies.

With a basic understanding of this alphabet, anyone can begin creating their own music and even explore more advanced music theory concepts. Whether you're just starting with your first instrument or want to hone your music writing skills, the music alphabet has all you need to get started.

Each letter refers to one of the different pitches, or tones, used to construct music. The **distance from one pitch to the next** (A to A♯ for example), is known as an **interval.** Intervals could also skip pitches, so that the distance from pitch A to D is also an interval. Chapter 3 goes into more detail on this.

In the music alphabet above, you will notice the following sign: ♯. It is not a 'hashtag'. In music, this is called a **sharp**. A sharp **raises** a pitch by a distance called a **half-step**. So the distance from A to A♯ is one half-step. Don't worry if this does not make sense yet – we will explore this in much more detail in Chapter 3.

You will also come across a symbol ♭ known as a **flat** sign. A flat is the opposite of a sharp - it **lowers** a pitch by a half-step.

Interestingly, the same music alphabet can also be written with flats (♭):

A - B♭ - B - C - D♭ - D - E♭ - E - F - G♭ - G - A♭
The music alphabet with flats ♭

The letters in the music alphabet are also called **notes.** Notice that the music alphabet above features flats instead of sharps. All sharpened notes in music can be written as a flattened note. For example, A♯ is the same pitch or note as B♭. We call this occurrence **enharmonic,** where two notes sound the same but are notated or spelled differently. C♯ is the same pitch or sound as D♭, and F♯ is the same pitch as G♭.

So, if we were to combine the two varieties of enharmonic, it would look like this:

A - A♯/B♭ - B - C - C♯/D♭ - D - D♯/E♭ - E - F - F♯/G♭ - G - G♯/A♭

You may wonder why we need multiple names for these sharpened and flattened notes. That's a great question! It's all due to scales and key signatures, which we will explore later in the book. For now, it's enough to understand that each sharpened (♯) note can also be called by its flat (♭) name, and vice versa.

Sharps (♯) and flats (♭) are known as **accidentals** in music. There's a third accidental called a **natural**, which looks like this ♮. If you see it in music, play the specific note in its original state, without it being a half-step higher or lower as a sharp or flat would denote.

The Music Alphabet

We now know there are twelve pitches in the music alphabet. But if you look at a piano, you can see more than twelve notes used in music. So, what are all these other notes?

The great thing about the music alphabet is that it repeats as the notes get higher or lower - to the end of your instrument or even the outer limits of human hearing!

The only letters you need to remember in music are A, B, C, D, E, F, and G. The frequency changes from one pitch to the next - so each one sounds unique and different.

When **repeated**, the music alphabet (using flats [♭] as an example) looks like this:

A - B♭ - B - C - D♭ - D - E♭ - E - F - G♭ - G - A♭ - A - B♭ - B - C - D♭ - D - E♭ - E - F - G♭ - G - A♭ - A - B♭ - B - C - D♭ - D - E♭ - E - F - G♭ - G - A♭ - A

The music alphabet in 3 octaves

Each iteration or repeat (starting at A, there are 3 in the example given) of the music alphabet is known as an **octave**. When we jump from one note to the next highest or lowest note of the **same name**, we jump by an octave. Hence A to the next A or D to the next D is a jump by an octave. Similarly, G♭ to the next G♭ or E♭ to the next E♭ is a jump by an octave.

Below is a keyboard showing the octave iterations from C to C. In the center is C4, more commonly referred to in piano circles as "middle C."

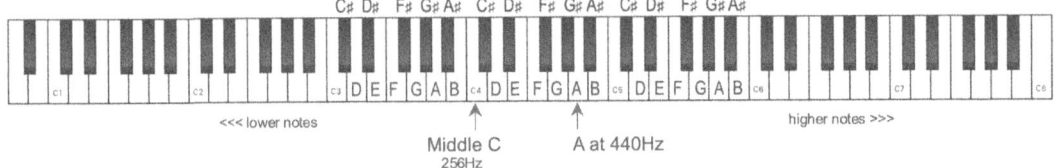

Keyboard showing 12 adjacent pitches across a music scale with sharps (♯)

The modern orchestra usually tunes to the pitch of A, which vibrates at a frequency of 440 Hertz. The A pitch that is one octave lower vibrates at a frequency of 220 Hertz. Meanwhile, the A one octave higher vibrates at a frequency of 880 Hertz. Moving up or down by an octave doubles or halves the note's frequency! As an aspiring musician, you need not concern yourself too much with frequency and Hertz - only that sounds you hear are pleasing (or not) to the ear.

Reading Music Notation

The ability to read music notation is a valuable skill for any musician. Even if you prefer to learn by ear, being able to read music allows you to easily express and share music with others, play music without first having to hear it, and understand the constructs of music on a deeper level.

Many beginner musicians shy away from learning to read notated music, believing it is too complicated and time-consuming a skill to master. But this is not the case. Reading music is logical, and there are several tricks we can use to help us. With regular practice, it is a skill anyone can master. Let's dive into the basic concepts.

The Staff

Traditionally, music is notated on a set of five horizontal lines known as the **staff**. Each line or space is assigned a note name.

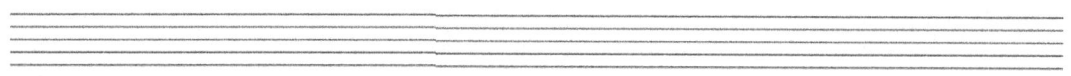

The position of each note on the staff indicates its pitch. Notes with a higher pitch appear higher on the staff, and notes with a lower pitch appear lower. Notes are written in both the lines and spaces of the staff, as shown:

<<< *lower pitch*   *higher pitch*>>>

Clefs

Clefs are the symbols we use to orient ourselves on the staff. They act as guideposts, telling us which lines and spaces correspond to which pitches. The clef always appears at the beginning of a piece of notated music.

While several clefs are used in music, in this book, we will focus only on the two most used: the treble clef and the bass clef.

The Treble Clef

The treble clef is an essential part of music notation. We'll look at how musicians use the treble clef to identify pitches on a musical staff, as well as some tips for mastering its use. With these tools, you can start reading music with confidence!

Treble Clef

The treble clef is used primarily for notes above middle C. It also corresponds to the right hand of the piano. Higher-pitched instruments like the flute, clarinet, and violin typically use the treble clef.

Like all clefs, the treble clef fixes the position of a specific pitch. But how do we know which pitch? Look at the round part in the middle of the treble clef symbol. See how it curls around the second line on the staff? This line is G. Hence the clef fixes the pitch of G at the second line position. For this reason, the treble clef is also known as the **G clef**.

Now that we know the position of G, we can figure out all the other pitches based on our knowledge of the music alphabet. Remember that notes move on the staff using the pattern of line, space, line, space, etc. Moving from G onto the space above it, we move to the next note in the music alphabet, A. From A, we step onto the next line and find B. From B we step to the next space, C, and so forth.

Here are the notes found on the treble clef staff:

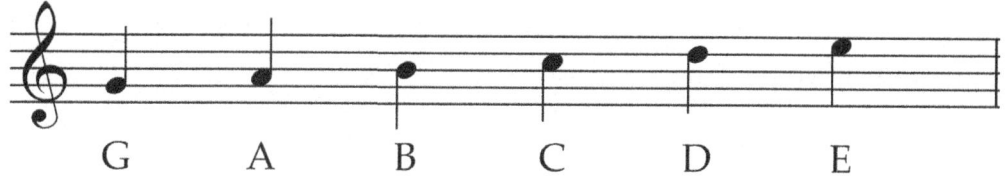

When we reach the top of the staff, we can add more notes using ledger lines, but we will get to that later in the book.

Learning the Notes of the Treble Clef

As mentioned earlier, we can use a few tricks and tools to memorize where the notes are found on the staff.

Generally, we break the notes up into those that appear on the lines:

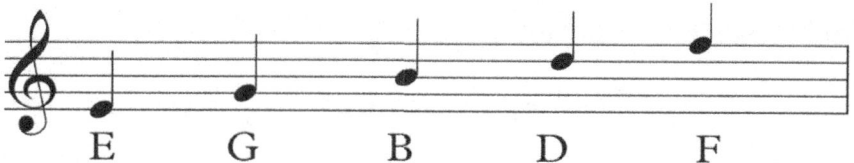

And those that appear in the spaces:

We use a mnemonic to learn and memorize where these notes lives. For the notes on the lines in the treble clef, we often use "**E**very **G**ood **B**oy **D**eserves **F**ruit," but feel free to make up your own if you will find it better.

For the notes in the spaces of the treble clef, we generally use "**FACE** in Space," simply because the notes in the spaces spell out the word FACE.

Treble Clef Practice

Let's practice identifying some notes on the treble clef. Use the above mnemonics to help you.

Here is the first example:

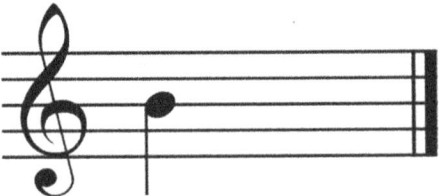

Firstly, determine whether this note is on a line or a space.

That's right; it is on a line.

Now, using the mnemonic Every Good Boy Deserves Fruit, count from the bottom to determine which line the note appears on.

It is on the third line – Every Good **Boy**; this is a B.

Great job.

Let's try another:

Again, the first step is determining whether the note is on a line or a space.

This one is in a space.

Now we count from the bottom and find it is in the fourth space.

Use the mnemonic FACE in Space – F, A, C, **E**; this is an E.

Don't worry if this feels time-consuming right now. With practice, it will become easier. With time, you will be able to recognize the notes simply by looking at them, in the same way you recognize and make sense of the words on this page.

The Bass Clef

The bass clef is commonly used in music notation to notate **lower-sounding** pitches, generally those below middle C.

Instruments with lower pitches such as the cello, trombone, and bass guitar, typically use the bass clef. It also corresponds to the left hand of the piano.

Bass Clef

Take a look at the bass clef. You will notice it begins on the fourth line from the bottom. There are also two dots, one on either side of this line. This line is where the note F lives (specifically, F below middle C). For this reason, the bass clef is also known as the F clef.

Learning the Notes of the Bass Clef

Just like with the earlier treble clef, we can use mnemonics to help memorize the notes of the bass clef. Again, dividing the notes into those on the lines and those in the spaces is helpful.

To memorize the notes on the lines in the bass clef, you can use the mnemonic "**G**ood **B**irds **D**on't **F**ly **A**way" – or create your own if it will help you remember.

The most commonly used mnemonic for the spaces of the left hand is "**All Cows Eat Grass**."

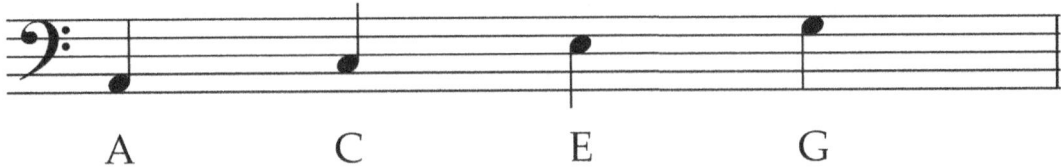

A   C   E   G

Bass Clef Practice

Let's practice identifying some notes in the bass clef. Here is your first example:

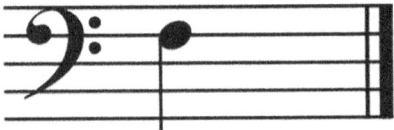

Remember that the first step is determining whether this note appears on a line or space.

Correct, it's on a line.

Now we count from the bottom to find it lives on the fourth line.

Refer to our mnemonic Good Birds Don't Fly Away – Good Birds Don't **Fly**; this note is F.

Let's try another example:

Is this note on a line or in a space?

That's right, it's in a space.

We count up from the bottom and find it is in the second space.

Now we use our mnemonic All Cows Eat Grass – All **Cows**; this note is C.

The Grand Staff

The treble and bass clef staffs are often combined to create the **grand staff**:

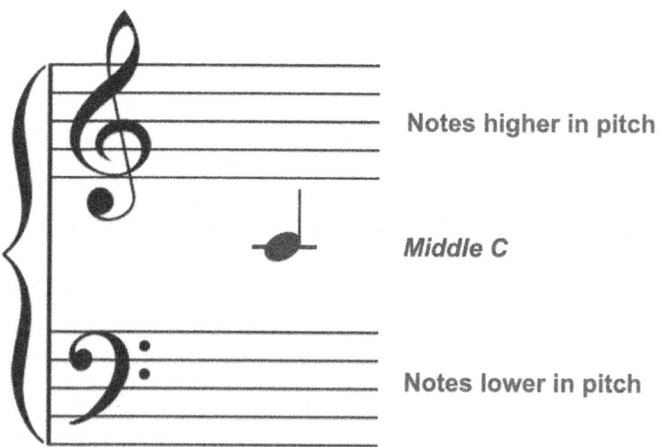

The grand staff is commonly used to notate piano music. The right hand plays the notes on the treble clef and the left plays the notes on the bass clef. The bracket connecting the two staffs indicates to be played together.

Here are the treble and bass clef notes notated on the grand staff:

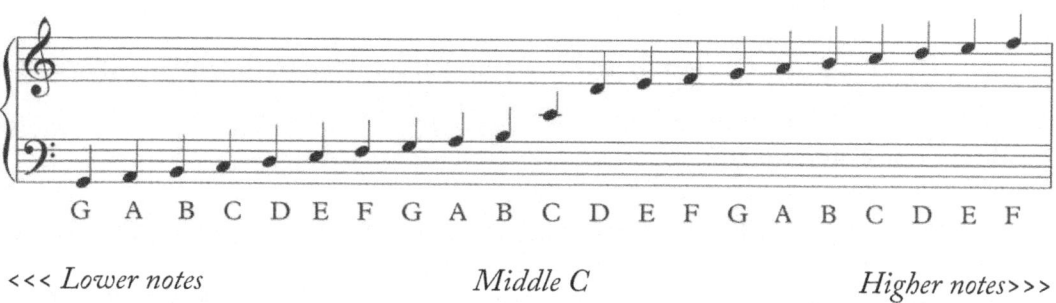

<<< *Lower notes*   *Middle C*   *Higher notes*>>>

The notes higher on the staff sound higher than notes found lower on the staff. You could compare it to a XY graph, where the X-axis is time or tempo (speed) of the music. Notes are played sequentially, one after the other, moving horizontally to the right. A music sheet reads from left to right. The Y-axis is the pitch moving up and down vertically on the staff from one note to the next.

Middle C

Look at the note right in the middle of the above grand staff. It is known as **middle C** because of its position on the staff. It also lies roughly in the middle of the piano.

Middle C appears at the top of the bass clef staff, and at the bottom of the treble clef staff. It is an easily recognizable note and can be used as a guidepost to identify the notes around it. If you take piano lessons, this is the first note you'll learn. It is also called as C4, because it is the 4th C note from the left on a standard 88-key piano keyboard.

Next, test what you've learned so far in this chapter.

Practice Time!

Use these questions and exercises to help practice your skills!

Chapter 1 Questions

1. What is the music alphabet? How many letters are in the music alphabet?
2. What is an octave?
3. What is the staff? How many lines are on the staff? How many spaces?
4. What does the treble clef tell us? How do we remember the notes on the lines and spaces of the treble clef?
5. What does the bass clef tell us? How do we remember the notes on the lines and spaces of the bass clef?
6. What is the grand staff?
7. Why is middle C called middle C?

Chapter 1 Exercises

1. Practice naming these notes in the treble clef:

2. Practice naming these notes in the bass clef:

3. Practice naming these notes on the grand staff:

4. First identify these pitches, then notate them one octave higher:

5. First identify these pitches, then notate them one octave lower:

Conclusion

In Chapter 1, we covered the basics of **pitch**. Pitch is the relative highness or lowness of a sound. The most common way to express pitch in music is with the **music alphabet**, but you can also measure pitch in frequency and Hertz.

A pitch is also called a note. There are twelve notes in the music alphabet repeated and extended higher or lower. Each time a letter name is repeated in the music alphabet, it is called an **octave**. Notes one octave apart are either **twice or half** the original note's frequency, depending on whether they are higher or lower. For example, the pitch A, one octave above A at 440 Hz (the tuning pitch of many orchestras) is 880 Hz, while the pitch A, one octave below A at 440 Hz is 220 Hz. Music is full of these sorts of interesting mathematical patterns.

Pitch is notated on a system of five lines and four spaces which we call **the staff**. The staff allows us to see the relative highness or lowness of pitches. Notes written higher on the staff are higher in pitch than those written lower on the staff. For example, the note on the fifth line of the staff is higher in pitch than the note on the first line, regardless of the clef.

Speaking of clefs, we use two basic clefs to orient ourselves on the staff. The first clef we learned is called the **treble clef**. The treble clef is primarily used **to notate pitches above middle C** and tells us the location of the pitch G (above middle C).

From there, we learned how to find the pitches in the treble clef. The second clef we learned about was the **bass clef**. The bass clef is primarily used **to notate pitches below middle C** and tells us the location of pitch F (below middle C). Likewise, we learned how to recognize the pitches in the bass clef.

Finally, we explored the combination of the treble and bass clef into the **grand staff**. The grand staff is commonly used to notate music for the piano as it adequately covers a wide range of pitches, which we can also extend using ledger lines. We learned that middle C is called such because it sits precisely in the middle of the grand staff.

It is essential to spend time practicing your reading skills. Do not expect to become a master reader overnight! But, with training, you can expect to become fluent in short order.

2
Exploring Rhythm

Keywords: rhythm, whole note, half note, quarter note, eighth note, whole rest, half rest, quarter rest, eighth rest, time signature, measure

What is Rhythm?

Rhythm is all around us. We can find rhythm in every corner of the universe. Your breathing moves in a rhythmic pattern, sometimes faster and sometimes slower. Your heart beats in a rhythmic pulse. You walk at various speeds, eat at different hours, and mark the passage of time throughout the days and years of life.

In a similar way, rhythm is the foundation of music. In its most basic form, rhythm is the perception of temporal patterns. It's the timing. It can be as simple as snapping your fingers or as complicated as your imagination allows. The principles of how rhythms function in music will seem obvious once you approach rhythm from this perspective.

Learning the fundamentals of rhythm is crucial if you want to understand music theory at a deep and profound level. Fortunately, it is not that complicated!

How is Rhythm Organized in Music?

Musical rhythm is structured using two main techniques: symbols called **notes** and **rests**, and **time signatures**.

Exploring Notes

We have already learned about notes. In addition to providing pitch information, notes are symbols that represent the **length of time** that a sound will last. The notes are categorized and measured using **time signatures**. Understanding how notes and time signatures work will expand your musical knowledge and allow you to be more creative in your musical compositions.

What Are the Different Types of Notes?

In essence, notes describe how long a sound lasts. There are a few main types of notes with some variations. Let's dive in.

Whole notes or semibreve last for **four counts** and looks like an empty oval. This blank oval is also called a notehead.

A whole note or semibreve

Half notes or minum last for **two counts**. It looks like a whole note with a stick alongside called a stem. When notated on the staff, this stem could point up or down.

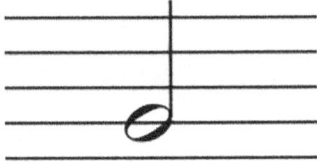

A half note or minum

Quarter notes or crotchet last for **one count**. It looks like a half note with the note head filled in.

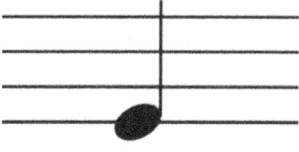

A quarter note or crotchet

Eighth notes or quaver lasts for **½ count**. It looks like a quarter note with a flag trailing from the stem.

An eighth note or quaver

Two eighth notes last for one count (½ + ½) and are often connected with a beam like this:

Sixteenth notes or semi-quaver are twice as fast as eighth notes and have two flags or beams instead of one. They last for **¼ of a beat** and look like this:

A sixteenth note or semi-quaver

Demi-semi-quaver notes or thirty-second notes are twice as fast as sixteenth notes and have three flags or beams. These last for 1/8 of a beat. You won't see them too often in music.

The Note Pyramid

The musical note pyramid or tree is a excellent way to visualize the note values and their relation to others. Each smaller note is precisely half the previous note.

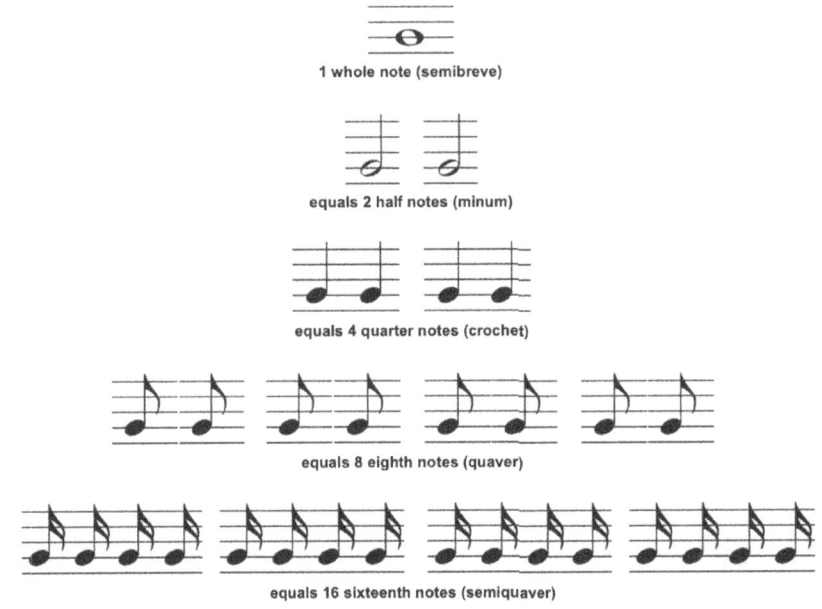

Music Note Pyramid

Observing the pyramid, you'll notice that notes seem to double or half in length, thus making it nicely divisible by two. It doesn't end here, though. Music notes can also be divisible by three, and to make it so, we add a dot (.) next to the note. The dot adds **half of the original** time value to the note length.

For example, adding a dot to a half note means taking its original value, namely two counts, and adding one count (half of two) to make it three counts. The same principle can be applied to all other notes, thus making them divisible by three.

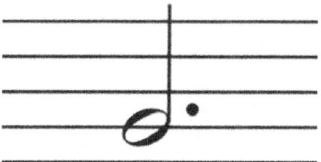

A dotted half note lasts for 3 counts

A division into thirds will affect the rhythmic pattern or beat of the music.

Rests: How Silence is Marked in Music

Just as we have symbols to mark sounds in music, we also have symbols to observe silence. In music, silence is just as important as sound. Without silence, would there be any such thing as sound? These pauses create contrast and brief moments of reflection or build anticipation of what's to come next.

We use symbols called **rests** to mark silence in music. There is an analogous rest for almost every type of note.

Name	Duration	Note Symbol	Rest Symbol
Whole	4 counts		
Half	2 counts		
Quarter	1 count		
Eighth	½ count		
Sixteenth	¼ count		

Whole rests and **half rests** look like rectangles, each positioned in the third space of the staff but affixed to the upper and lower line, respectively.

The **quarter rest** is a sort of 'Z' shape with a 'c' attached to the bottom. It generally sits between the second and fourth lines of the staff. Like the quarter note, it lasts for one count.

The **eighth rest** resembles a stylized '7' and likewise sits between the second and fourth lines of the staff. Like the eighth note, it lasts for ½ count.

The **sixteenth rest** is the same shape as the eighth rest, with an additional flag attached to it, similar to the two beams of the sixteenth note. Like the sixteenth note, the sixteenth rest lasts a ¼ of a count.

How do Time Signatures Affect Notes?

Besides pitch and a note's length, rhythm or beat is essential to drive the music forward. Without it, it's simply sound. It's not music.

A **time signature** specifies how many counts or beats are contained within one measure, and the type of note that will serve as the counting unit.

Measures act like containers that hold the beats of a piece of music. All music pieces contain measures in some form. Vertical lines on a staff separate one measure from the other. These lines are called **bar lines** or **measure lines.**

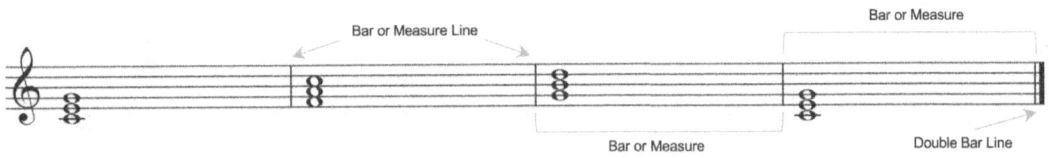

The distance from one vertical line to another is a bar or measure

The following are examples of a few different time signatures:

'Four-four" time signature

Exploring Rhythm

"Three-four" time signature

"Six-eight" time signature

The time signature's **top number** indicates the number of counts within each measure. If the top number is 4, four counts will be in one measure. If the top number is 3, there will be three counts. If the top number is 6, there will be six counts. These are the most basic and common numbers, but there are many more.

The **bottom number** indicates the type of note used as the basic unit of counting. If the bottom number is 4, a quarter note equals one count. If the bottom number is 8, the eighth note equals one count.

Here are some more **time signatures** and their **counting rhythm** to familiarize yourself:

$\frac{2}{4}$	Two quarter beats per measure counted "one, two, one two" and typically found in marches
$\frac{3}{4}$	Three quarter beats per measure counted "one, two, three, one two, three"
$\frac{4}{4}$	Four quarter beats per measure, also known as Common Time, indicated with a C
$\frac{5}{4}$	Five quarter beats per measure played a lot in jazz music
$\frac{3}{8}$	Three eighth beats per measure
$\frac{6}{8}$	Six eighth beats per measure, the rhythm feels like a waltz ¾ timing
$\frac{9}{8}$	Nine eighth beats per measure, again feels like a waltz rhythm

The bottom number of a time signature will most commonly be 4 or 8, but you might see 16 at the bottom in more advanced music. You might also see 2 which denotes half-notes. If you are extremely daring, you can look up irrational meters and prepare to have your mind blown!

Feel the Rhythm

If you have never had a practical use for the knowledge, reading about the various types of notes and time signatures may seem abstract or arcane right now. So, here's a quick activity to help you absorb these patterns.

Create pathways for yourself using the various note lengths, then count aloud and clap your way through them. Let's start with $\frac{4}{4}$ timing which denotes four quarter notes per bar.

Count and clap each note on beats 1, 2, 3, 4. If you have a metronome, use this to help maintain a steady, even pace. An online version is also findable. Set the metronome timer at 80 beats per minute (BPM), a moderately paced tempo (speed) with an easy, natural feel.

By starting slowly, you'll begin feeling the movement of the beat and understand the rhythm for yourself. For $\frac{4}{4}$ timing, count 1, 2, 3, 4 for each click sound of the metronome, which will correspond to a quarter note.

$$1, 2, 3, 4, 1, 2, 3, 4...$$

Repeat the sequence over and over. Do you feel the beat? It's even and steady.

These quarter beats can be subdivided into eighth notes. One quarter note equals two eighth notes. The counting will go like this.

$$\text{1- and, 2- and, 3- and, 4- and, 1- and, 2- and, 3- and, 4- and, ...}$$

Maintaining the same 80-BPM tempo, again repeat the sequence over and over. The beat is still quarter notes, but there are now 8 notes altogether in a bar shown with the addition of the "and". These are called **off-beats** which are notes in between the main beats 1, 2, 3, 4. Maintain the same speed as in the previous exercise by clapping on each beat but say "and" when your hand opens between the beats. Same speed but the rhythm changes.

Sub-dividing further still into sixteenth notes and the counting goes like this:

$$1\text{- e - and - a, 2- e - and - a, 3- e - and - a, 4- e - and - a, ...}$$

You'll notice more off-beats added, namely the 'e' and the 'a'. Each quarter note beat adds up to 4 sixteenth notes in the form of 1 - ee - and - ay.

With 4 beats to a bar, the total number of eighth notes will be 16 per bar. A reminder that the click of the metronome (or your clap) corresponds to the numerals 1, 2, 3, 4.

Did you feel how the rhythm changes? Consider it like shifting gears in a car or on a bike. Each level serves a different purpose and has a different feel and meaning.

Let's jump to the $\frac{3}{4}$ time signature showing 3 quarter notes per bar. The counting will look like this:

$$1, 2, 3, 1, 2, 3, 1, 2, 3,...$$

Change the metronome time to 90 beats per minute and count 1, 2, 3, 1, 2, 3...

Does this feel familiar? If it does, you'll know it's the rhythmic pattern for a waltz dance.

How about $\frac{2}{4}$ timing? Change the metronome time to 120 beats per minute and count:

$$1, 2, 1, 2, 1, 2, 1, 2...$$

When listening to a drum section, did you ever feel an "oom-pah oom-pah" rhythmic feel? You probably have. This is $\frac{2}{4}$ time signature, which is also the rhythmic feel for a marching band song.

If you think of notes, time signatures, and measures as building blocks, some exciting rhythms and patterns are created that you might not have otherwise composed.

Practice Time!

Use these questions and exercises to help practice your skills!

Chapter 2 Questions

1. What is rhythm? What are the two essential tools musicians use to organize rhythm in music?

2. What are the various notes and their durations? How many quarter notes equal a whole note? How many eighth notes equal one quarter note?

3. What is a dotted note?

4. What are rests? What are the various rests and their durations? How long does a quarter rest last? How many quarter rests equal one whole rest?

5. What is a time signature, and what do musicians use it for? What does the top number of the time signature tell us? What about the bottom number?

6. How many beats are in a measure in $\frac{4}{4}$ time signature? What about a $\frac{6}{8}$ time signature?

Chapter 2 Exercises

1. Identify the following types of notes:

2. Identify the following types of rests:

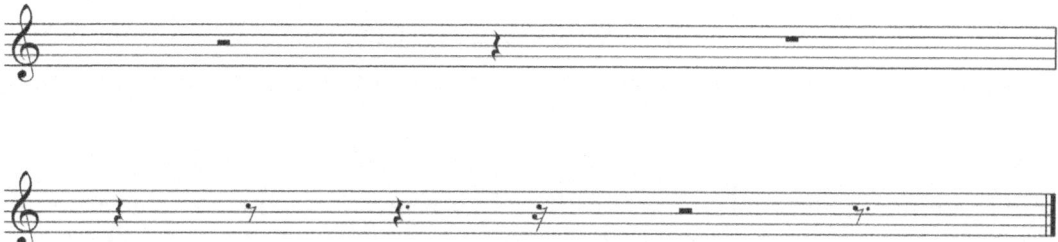

3. Practice filling in the measures with the appropriate number of notes and or rests:

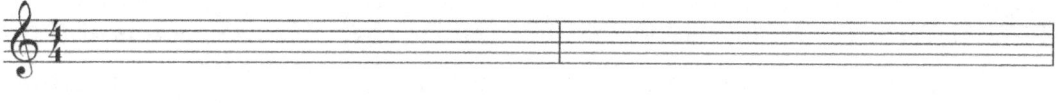

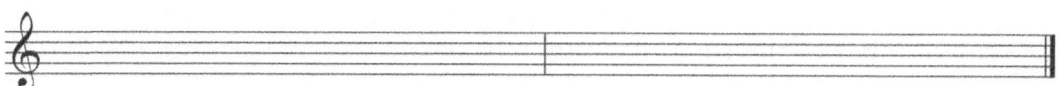

4. Try the same exercise but in $\frac{6}{8}$ time signature:

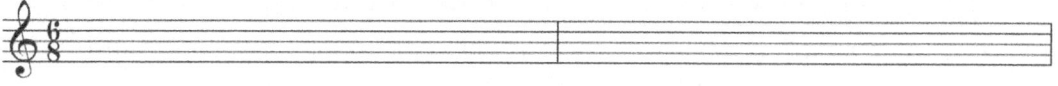

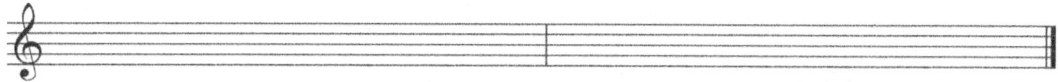

5. Fill in the missing rhythms using notes or rests in a 3/4 time signature:

Conclusion

Rhythm is all around us. We see rhythm in the sunrise and sunset, feel rhythms in our heartbeats and breath, and hear rhythms in music. We communicate rhythm in music, primarily using **note** and **rest** symbols and **time signatures.**

The shapes and qualities of notes and rests give us information about the duration of sound or silence. Each of these symbols represents a quantifiable amount of time that usually is evenly divisible. The essential durations are **whole note/rest, half note/rest, quarter note/rest, eighth note/rest,** and **sixteenth note/rest.** We also use the **dot symbol** next to a note to increase its value by ½ of its original duration.

Time signatures are the tool we use to organize rhythms into **groups of time** called **measures.** Measures are the basic building blocks of musical notation and its central organizing principle.

The **top number** of the time signature tells us how many beats are inside one measure. For example, if the top number is 4, all the notes inside one measure will add up to 4.

The **bottom number** tells us which type of note will receive one count. For example, if the bottom number is 4, the quarter note will receive one count. If the bottom number is 8, eighth notes will receive one count. You will encounter 4 or 8 as the likely bottom notes in a time signature.

Finally, we explored some basic exercises and combinations of rhythms and time signatures. Look at examples of your favorite music written in musical notation and see if you can identify elements like the time signature, measures, different note lengths, and durations. Even better, see if you can follow along on the page and count as you listen to the music on a recording!

Have fun and enjoy this practice.

3

Exploring Intervals

Keywords: interval, half-step, whole step, semitone, whole tone, major, minor, second, third, perfect fourth, perfect fifth, augmented, diminished, sixth, seventh, octave

What is an Interval?

The distance between pitches or notes is called an interval and measured in units called a half-step or a whole step. A whole step consists of two half-steps.

A half-step is the distance from one note to **the next highest or lowest note**. So looking at the musical alphabet (in sharps ♯) again:

A - A♯ - B - C - C♯ - D - D♯ - E - F - F♯ - G - G♯
The musical alphabet with sharps ♯

The distance from A to A♯ is a **half-step**, similarly the distance from C♯ to D or E to F. It also works in the opposite direction so that B is a half-step below C and G is a half-step below G♯.

An instrument that shows this well is the guitar, where moving from one fret to the next is the distance of a half-step.

On a piano keyboard, a half-step distance is moving from one key to the very next one, whether such key is white or black. Again, this works whether one moves in a left or right direction up or down the keyboard.

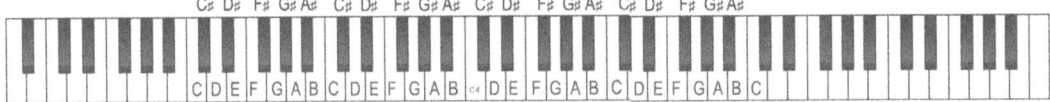

Keys or notes on a piano keyboard half-step interval apart.

On the grand staff, using the examples of E and B as starting point, it would look like this:

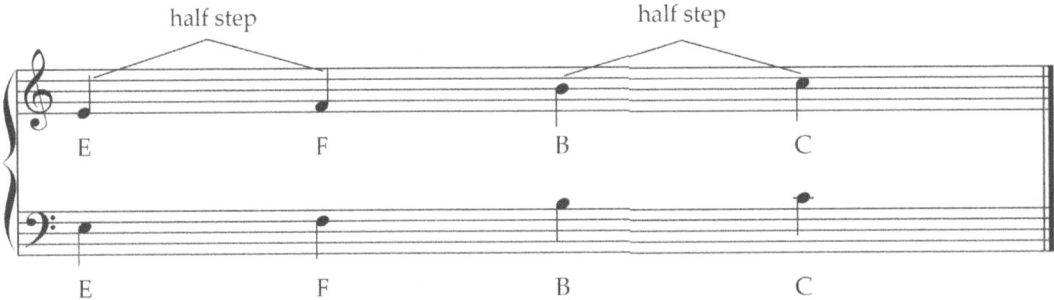

The next important term is **whole step**. A whole step is the distance of **two half-steps, either up or down.**

Looking at the musical alphabet again, the distance from C to D is a whole step because it's two half-steps apart. C to C♯ is a half-step apart, and so is C♯ to D.

Similarly, the distance from E to F♯ or G to F is equal to a whole step as two half-steps separates them.

Another term for half-step and whole step is semitone and whole tone respectively. Throughout this book, we use half-step (H) and whole step (W) but on your music journey, be aware that other references exist.

Let's test your knowledge of half-step and whole step terminology using the musical alphabet in flats.

A - B♭ - B - C - D♭ - D - E♭ - E - F - G♭ - G - A♭

The musical alphabet with flats ♭

Exploring Intervals

A half-step is the distance from one note to **the next highest or lowest note**, from any note to the next, for example, B♭ to B or D♭ to D or G to G♭ or F to E.

A whole step is the distance of two half-steps, as in the distance from B to D♭ or E♭ to D♭ or G♭ to A♭.

But there are distances greater than a half-step or whole step. How do we describe these distances?

The Distance Between Notes

We describe intervals greater than a half-step or whole step by using a combination of descriptive words and numbers. The words include **major, minor, perfect** and **augmented,** and the number indicates how far apart the notes are.

For example, any interval in which the notes are **two letter names** apart, F to G for example, is called an **interval of a second**. Any interval that moves from one note to the next in the music alphabet, will be called a **second.**

Again, have a look at the music alphabet to test these concepts.

A - B♭ - B - C - D♭ - D - E♭ - E - F - G♭ - G - A♭

The musical alphabet with flats ♭

With closer inspection though, one sees that there are two possible choices for an interval of a second above F. We could choose G or G♭. This is where the terms **major** and **minor** come into play. The interval distance of F to G♭ is called a **minor second** (one half-step), and the interval of F to G is called a **major second** (two half-steps).

The interval from F to A is **three letters apart (F – G – A),** so any interval distance three letters apart, is an **interval of a third**. Again, we have two possible choices - one could choose F to A♭ (three half-steps) or F to A (four half-steps). F to A♭ is called a **minor third** and the interval from F to A is called a **major third**. Make sense?

Any interval distance **four letter names** apart, C to F for example, is called an **interval of a fourth.**

This might seem a little confusing at first, but the more you look at it, the easier it becomes. With practice, you will be able to look at any interval on the staff and know exactly what it is without having to think about it, just like you read the signs on the road or the items on a menu.

As music moves from one note to the next, it does so in intervals creating the melody or harmony of music. The various interval names inside of one octave and their corresponding number of half-steps are below. Knowing these terms will prove helpful when communicating ideas to other musicians.

Interval	No. of Half Steps
Unison	0
Minor Second	1
Major Second	2
Minor Third	3
Major Third	4
Perfect Fourth	5
Augmented Fourth	6
Perfect Fifth	7
Minor Sixth	8
Major Sixth	9
Minor 7th	10
Major 7th	11
Octave	12

Intervals on the Music Staff

Viewed on the staff, here are all the interval names inside of one octave and their corresponding number of half-steps. C is used as starting point; however, it applies to any note.

Unison - 0 half-steps - C to C

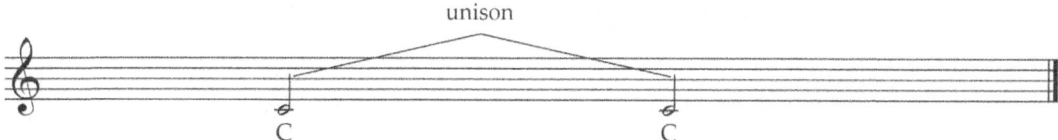

Minor second - 1 half-step - C to D♭

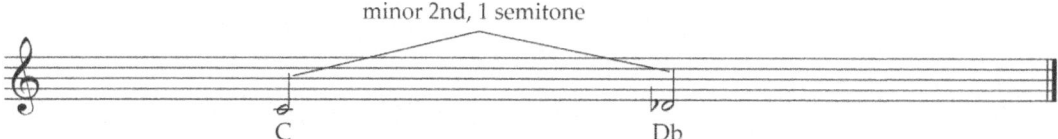

Major second - 2 half-steps - C to D

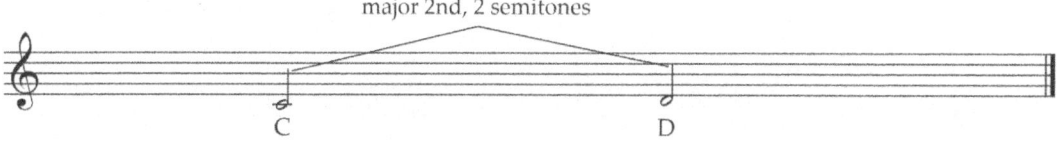

Minor third - 3 half-steps - C to E♭

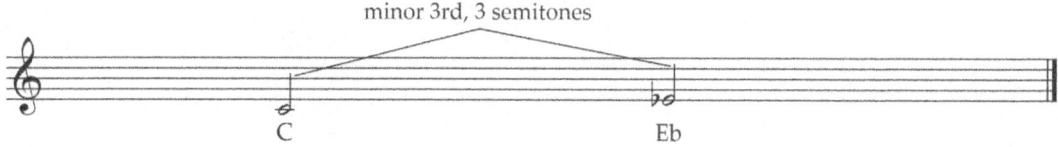

Major third - 4 half-steps - C to E

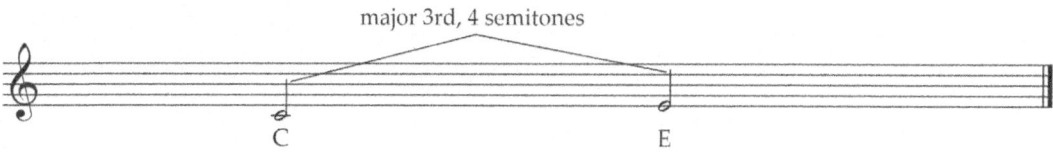

Perfect fourth - 5 half-steps - C to F

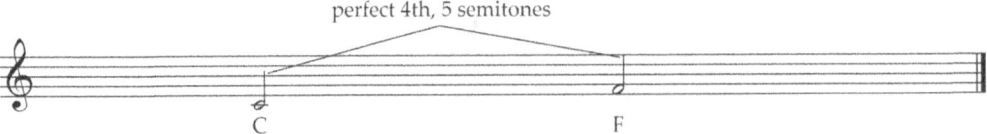

Augmented fourth 6 half-steps - C to F♯

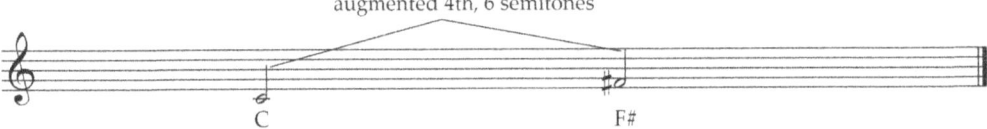

Perfect fifth - 7 half-steps - C to G

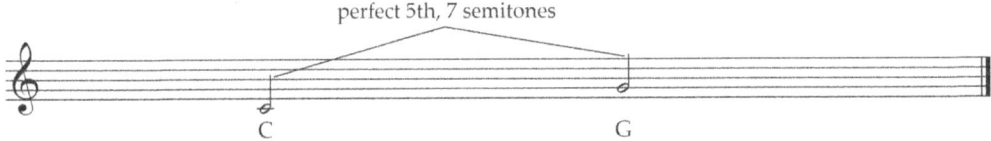

Minor sixth - 8 half-steps - C to A♭

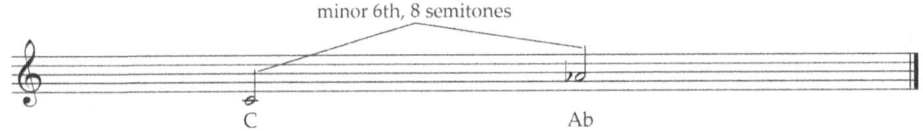

Major sixth - 9 half-steps - C to A

Exploring Intervals

Minor seventh - 10 half-steps - C to B♭

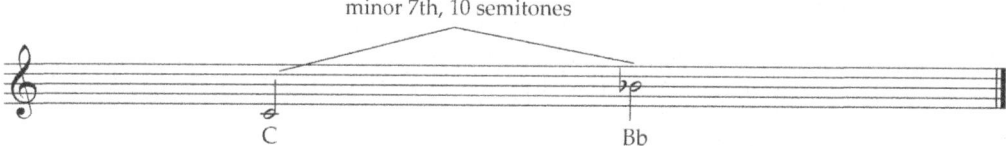

Major seventh - 11 half-steps - C to B

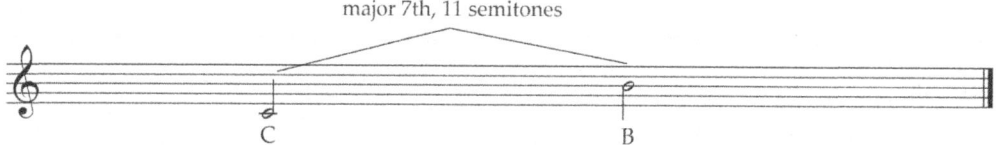

One octave - 12 half-steps - C to C

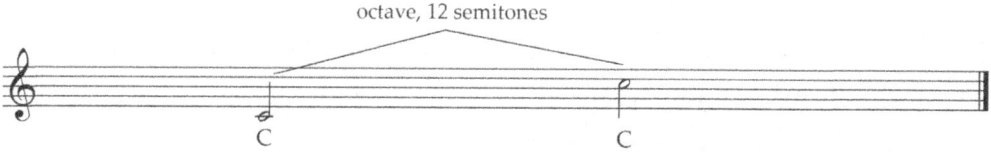

Here are some practice examples you can use to build your skills in measuring intervals. Count the half-steps between the notes and consult the table above for its correct name.

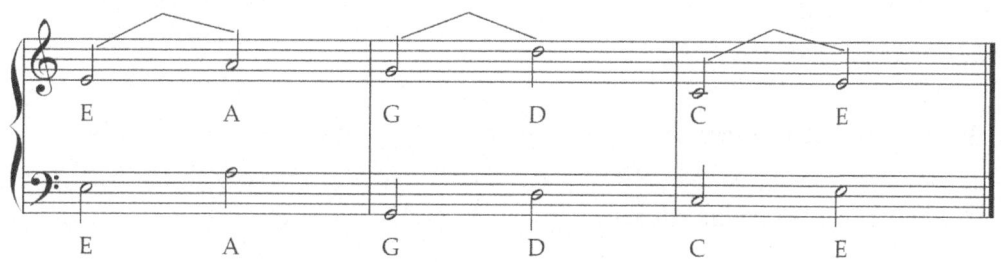

The intervals shown on the staff are:

- E to A is a **perfect fourth.** Start at E and move to F, F♯, G, G♯, A = 5 half-steps

- G to D is a **perfect fifth.** Start at G and move to G♯, A, A♯, B, C, C♯, D = 7 half-steps

- C to E is a **major third.** Start at C and move to C♯, D, D♯, E = 4 half-steps

Melodic vs. Harmonic Intervals

Intervals appear in two ways in music: as **melodic intervals** and as **harmonic intervals**.

Melodic intervals appear **sequentially**. A melodic minor second interval means note C moves to D♭ in a melody. They are played one after the other in sequence - not simultaneously.

A harmonic minor second interval means that C and D♭ are **played at the same time,** as in a **chord.** All intervals can be either melodic or harmonic, depending on the context or the composer's choice.

You'll learn more about chords in Chapter 5.

Practice Time!

Chapter 3 Questions

1. What is an interval?

2. How are intervals measured?

3. How many half-steps are in a minor third? What about a perfect fifth? How about a minor seventh?

4. What is a melodic interval? A harmonic interval?

Exploring Intervals

Chapter 3 Exercises

1. Practice writing the following intervals:

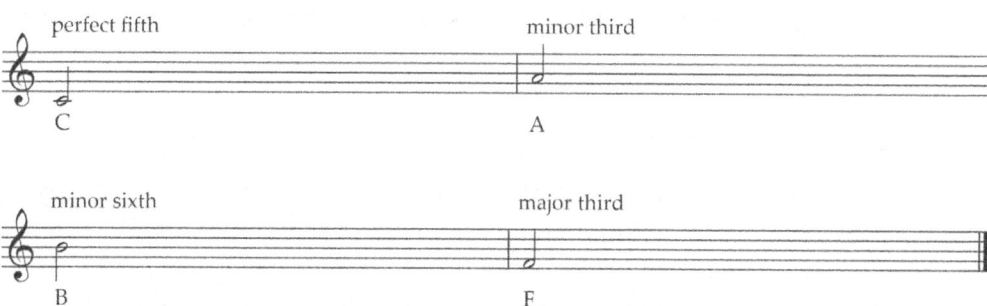

2. Practice identifying the following intervals:

Conclusion

In Chapter 3, we explored the concept of music intervals. An interval is simply the distance between two notes, whether side by side or multiple steps away. We measure intervals in basic units called **half steps** or **whole steps.** Two half-steps equal one whole step. Another term for a half-step and whole step is a semitone and whole tone respectively.

We explored all the possible interval relationships from C and found that twelve exist inside one octave (C to C). We introduced words like **unison, minor, major, perfect, augmented,** and **octave** in conjunction with a numerical value to describe these intervals.

For example, the distance from C to F is a perfect fourth (five half-steps), the distance from C to A is a major sixth (nine half-steps), and the distance from C to E♭ is a minor third (three half-steps). Study, memorize, and practice with the diagrams in this chapter, and you will gain a better understanding of how to measure intervals.

You can likewise take examples from any notated versions of your favorite songs and measure the intervals in the melody. This is a great way to apply music theory to your favorite music immediately.

If you want to hear what the intervals sound like, try an online piano keyboard like https://www.musicca.com/piano. You'll find the notes written on the keyboard, so you'll have no problem finding them.

4
Exploring Scales

Keywords: scales, major scale, minor scale, interval, semitone, whole tone, whole step, half step, scale degrees, major, minor, relative major, relative minor, pentatonic, chromatic, whole step scale

Combine Pitches and Intervals to Build Scales

In Chapter 3, you learned that an **interval** is simply the distance between two notes.

In this chapter, we will begin to explore the world of scales. A music **scale** is a set of notes within an octave arranged and played sequentially according to their pitch. Most scales have seven notes in a scale. Others, like the pentatonic scale, may only have five.

The ascending or descending interval relationships among the pitches define each scale. We derive a generic formula from this relationship for transposing the scale to different keys (*you'll learn about keys in Chapter 6*). Moreover, the notes from a scale played in various ways will form **melodies** and **harmonies**, which you hear when you listen to a tune.

There are several types of scales. The two main types are the **major scale** and the **natural minor scale**.

You can build both major and minor scales from any note. The note you start on is called the "root" note or the "tonic."

The type of scale is determined by the **pattern of intervals** in a combination of half-steps and whole steps. Let's explore these patterns!

Using Intervals to Build the Major Scale

The major scale is one of the most common scales in music. It consists of seven notes following the interval pattern of whole steps and half-steps:

whole - whole - half - whole - whole - whole - half

Steps

All major scales follow this interval pattern and formula. Memorize this pattern, and you can build a major scale starting from any note.

Let's try to build a few of them to get a feel for how it works. We will start with the C Major scale, which is commonly the first scale beginner pianists learn. We will use the interval formula above to build the C Major scale.

Here's the musical alphabet as a reference. With more notes added, it's longer, so we see a full octave range from C to C.

A - A♯ - B - C - C♯ - D - D♯ - E - F - F♯ - G - G♯ - A - A♯ - B - C - C♯ - D - D♯ - E

Octave (12 half-steps)

If we begin with C and move up one whole step, we reach D. If we move up one whole step from D, we reach E. One half-step above E is F. One whole step above F is G. One whole step above G is A. One whole step above A is B. And finally, one half-step above B is C.

Exploring Scales

Put another way:

Pitch	Interval Distance
C to D	Whole step
D to E	Whole step
E to F	Half-step
F to G	Whole step
G to A	Whole step
A to B	Whole step
B to C	Half-step

Intervals of a Major scale

This means the C Major scale is written as C - D - E - F - G - A - B - C. Simple, right? See how the notes are shown one after the other according to the musical alphabet? Playing on the piano starting on the note C, you play all the white keys.

Check out the C Major scale notated in the treble clef below:

And the C Major scale notated in the bass clef:

It is as simple as that. Now, start on any of the 12 notes in the music alphabet, apply the scale interval formula, and you've created a major scale from the note you started on.

Here are all the major scales containing either sharps or flats. Later in Chapter 6 you'll see the order of adding sharps or flats in reference to key signatures and the Circle of Fifths.

Major Scale (with ♯)	1	2	3	4	5	6	7
C Major (0)	C	D	E	F	G	A	B
G Major (1♯)	G	A	B	C	D	E	F♯
D Major (2♯)	D	E	F♯	A	B	C♯	D
A Major (3♯)	A	B	C♯	D	E	F♯	G♯
E Major (4♯)	E	F♯	G♯	A	B	C♯	D♯
B Major (5♯)	B	C♯	D♯	E	F♯	G♯	A♯
F♯ Major (6♯)	F♯	G♯	A♯	B	C♯	D♯	E♯
C♯ Major (7♯)	C♯	D♯	E♯	F♯	G♯	A♯	B♯
Major Scale (with ♭)							
F Major (1♭)	F	G	A	B♭	C	D	E
B♭ Major (2♭)	B♭	C	D	E♭	F	G	A
E♭ Major (3♭)	E♭	F	G	A♭	B♭	C	D
A♭ Major (4♭)	A♭	B♭	C	D♭	E♭	F	G
D♭ Major (5♭)	D♭	E♭	F	G♭	A♭	B♭	C
G♭ Major (6♭)	G♭	A♭	B♭	C♭	D♭	E♭	F
C♭ Major (7♭)	C♭	D♭	E♭	F♭	G♭	A♭	B♭

Major scales with scale degrees 1-7

Notice that the C♯ Major and D♭ Major scales are the same notes, but one is a scale written in sharps and the other in flats. The same applies to F♯ Major and G♭ Major.

The major scale is a neutral, happy, and bright-sounding scale full of easy and clear resolution points.

Whatever instrument you choose to play, knowing these basic building blocks is essential. The same applies to the natural minor scale, which you'll learn about next.

Using Intervals to Build the Minor Scale

The minor scale also consists of seven notes with a unique interval pattern between them. There are three types of minor scales, natural, harmonic, and melodic. Unlike major scales, the minor scale sounds sad, darker, solemn, or ominous. This is due to the minor third interval between the 1st and 3rd degree of the scale.

Natural Minor Scale

The natural minor scale follows this pattern of whole steps and half-steps:

Whole - Half - Whole - Whole - Half - Whole - Whole
Steps

Memorize this pattern and build a natural minor scale starting from any note. Let's try from the note A to see how it works.

Here's the musical alphabet as a reference in flats (♭), showing an octave range from A to A.

A - B♭ - B - C - D♭ - D - E♭ - E - F - G♭ - G - A♭ - A - B♭ - B - C - D♭ - D - E♭ - E

Octave (12 half-steps)

If we begin with A and move up one whole step, we reach B. If we move up one half-step from B, we reach C. One whole step above C is D. One whole step above D is E. One half-step above E is F. One whole step above F is G. And finally, one whole step above G is A.

Put another way:

Pitch	Interval Distance
A to B	Whole step
B to C	Half-step
C to D	Whole step
D to E	Whole step
E to F	Half-step
F to G	Whole step
G to A	Whole step

Intervals of Natural Minor scale

The A natural minor scale is therefore written as A - B - C - D - E - F - G. Check out the A natural minor scale notated in the treble clef below:

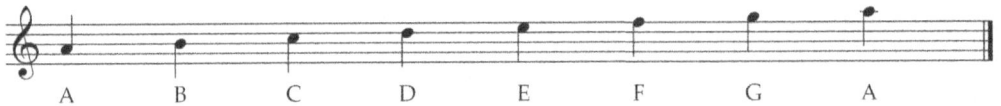

And here it is notated in the bass clef:

It is as simple as that. Now, start on any of the 12 notes in the music alphabet, apply the natural minor scale interval formula, and you've created a natural minor scale for the note you started on.

For now, here's a quick reference chart displaying all the natural minor scales:

Minor Scale (with ♯)	1	2	3	4	5	6	7
A Minor (0)	A	B	C	D	E	F	G
E Minor (1♯)	E	F♯	G	A	B	C	D
B Minor (2♯)	B	C♯	D	E	F♯	G	A
F♯ Minor (3♯)	F♯	G♯	A	B	C♯	D	E
C♯ Minor (4♯)	C♯	D♯	E	F♯	G♯	A	B
G♯ Minor ((5♯)	G♯	A♯	B	C♯	D♯	E	F♯
D♯ Minor (6♯)	D♯	E♯	F♯	G♯	A♯	B	C♯
A♯ Minor (7♯)	A♯	B♯	C♯	D♯	E♯	F♯	G♯
Minor Scale (with ♭)							
D Minor (1♭)	D	E	F	A	B♭	C	D
G Minor (2♭)	G	A	B♭	C	D	E♭	F
C Minor (3♭)	C	D	E♭	F	G	A♭	B♭
F Minor (4♭)	F	G	A♭	B♭	C	D♭	E♭
B♭ Minor (5♭)	B♭	C	D♭	E♭	F	G♭	A♭
E♭ Minor (6♭)	E♭	F	G♭	A♭	B♭	C♭	D♭
A♭ Minor (7♭)	A♭	B♭	C♭	D♭	E♭	F♭	G♭

Natural Minor Scales with Scale Degrees

Harmonic Minor Scale

This scale is like the natural minor scale, except the seventh note is raised by a half-step. G♯ is the seventh note raised in the example below, showing the A harmonic minor scale. The A harmonic minor scale is a frequently used scale on a guitar.

Pitch	Interval Distance
A to B	Whole step
B to C	Half-step
C to D	Whole step
D to E	Whole step
E to F	Half-step
F to G♯	Whole step + Half-step
G♯ to A	Half-step

Intervals of Harmonic Minor scale

Melodic Minor Scale

Again, this scale is like the natural minor scale, except that the melodic minor scale raises both the sixth and seventh notes of the natural minor scale.

In the example below showing the A melodic minor scale, the sixth and seventh note is raised by a half-step, resulting in F♯ and G♯, respectively.

Pitch	Interval
A to B	Whole step
B to C	Half-step
C to D	Whole step
D to E	Whole step
E to F♯	Whole step
F♯ to G♯	Whole step
G♯ to A	Half-step

Intervals of Melodic Minor scale

Pentatonic, Chromatic and Whole Tone Scales

There are some other scales called pentatonic, chromatic, and whole tone. Penta means "five", hence a **pentatonic** scale has only **5 notes** comprising the tonic, supertonic, mediant, dominant, and submediant. More on these terms a little further on.

The **chromatic scale** is a **12-note** scale and comprises only intervals of half-steps. Start on any note, play a half-step above, and continue this pattern until you reach the note letter name you started on. It's also known as the master scale, containing all the notes from which all other scales are built.

The **whole tone** scale is a **6-note** scale comprising only intervals of whole tones.

Scale Degrees

Every tone or pitch in a scale has a number associated with it. This number is known as the **scale degree**. A scale degree is a number showing the **ordinal position** of a note in a scale.

For example, in the C Major scale, we label C as 1, D as 2, E as 3, F as 4, G as 5, A as 6, and B as 7. This means that D is the second scale degree, E is the third, F is the fourth, and so forth.

1	2	3	4	5	6	7
C	D	E	F	G	A	B

C Major with scale degrees

Generally, we learn the C Major scale first because it is a neutral canvas that we can mold and transform. The C Major scale has only natural (no sharps or flats) scale degrees 1 - 7. All the other scale degree formulations are made relative to this formula.

The number of degrees in a scale depends on how many notes it has. For example, some scales only have five scale degrees because they have only five notes (such as the pentatonic scale). However, the scale degrees still need to be labeled as relative to the scale degrees of the major scale. This way, all of our formulas remain cohesive with one another.

Scale degrees are an effective way of communicating information about scales to other musicians. They offer a generic form of sharing information that can then apply to different scales and situations. For example, if you know that a particular melodic passage goes 3 - 4 - 6 - 5, you can use that information to play it in all twelve keys.

Understanding Relative Major and Relative Natural Minor

Relative Minor

The relationship between the major and natural minor scales is called the relative minor or relative major. There is a relative minor scale for every major scale, and for every minor scale, there is a relative major. The notes of the major scale and its corresponding natural minor scale are **identical** and vice versa. The difference is the **starting note** of the scale.

The relative minor of a major scale starts on the sixth degree of the major scale. Let's apply the principle to the E♭ major scale.

1	2	3	4	5	6	7
E♭	F	G	A♭	B♭	C	D

E♭ Major with scale degrees

C is the sixth degree of the E♭ major scale; hence the relative natural minor scale will start on C and have the exact same tones as the E♭ major scale, namely

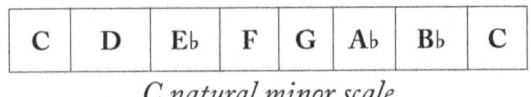

C natural minor scale

Exploring Scales

Let's try another example. What will the relative minor be if we are in the key of F Major? Check out the F Major scale notated below in the treble clef:

Starting from F, count up to six notes. F - G - A - Bb - C - D. D is the sixth scale degree of F major. D minor, therefore is the relative minor of F major, and D minor is the relative minor scale.

Check out the D minor scale notated below:

Notice how it has the same notes as the F Major scale? Now let's explore the relative major.

Relative Major

Now that you understand the concept of relative minor reasonably well, let's look at **relative major.** Relative major is simply the opposite of relative minor. For every minor scale, there is a relative major scale.

The relative major scale of any minor scale starts on the **third degree** of the minor scale. Let's use the A natural minor scale to test the principle.

1	2	3	4	5	6	7
A	B	C	D	E	F	G

A natural minor scale

C is the third degree of the A natural minor scale. And we already know that C major is the relative major of A minor.

But let's try a slightly more obscure example and see if we can practice building the natural minor scale along the way.

Let's use the G minor scale. Can you build the G minor scale using the formula and interval pattern we learned in this chapter? Remember the formula for a natural minor scale is:

Whole - Half - Whole - Whole - Half - Whole - Whole
Steps

Starting from G, count up one whole step to A, one half-step to Bb, one whole step to C, one whole step to D, one half-step to Eb, one whole step to F, and finally, one whole step back to G.

1	2	3	4	5	6	7
G	A	Bb	C	D	Eb	F

G natural minor scale

Check it out notated below on the staff.

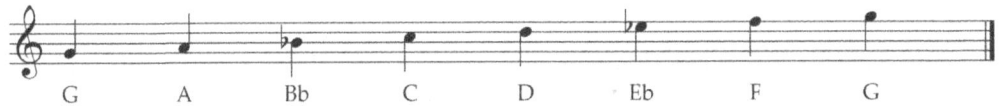

Now that you have the minor scale, you can quickly identify that Bb is the third degree which is the position the relative major scale will start from. Bb is therefore the relative major of G minor. Easy, right?

You may be wondering why should you know all this? Well, one reason is that if ever you find yourself in the exciting world of improvisation, it is essential to know. Moving between relative major and minor will give you more range and ideas on what notes to play while improvising.

Here's a handy reference for relative major and minor scales. In Chapter 6 you'll discover a music wheel called the Circle of Fifths which also shows this along with other essential data musicians find highly useful.

Relative Major	Relative Minor	Sharps / Flats
C	A	-
G	E	F♯
D	B	F♯ C♯
A	F♯	F♯ C♯ G♯
E	C♯	F♯ C♯ G♯ D♯
B	G♯	F♯ C♯ G♯ D♯ A♯
F♯	D♯	F♯ C♯ G♯ D♯ A♯ E♯
C♯	A♯	F♯ C♯ G♯ D♯ A♯ E♯ B♯
F	D	B♭
B♭	G	B♭ E♭
E♭	C	B♭ E♭ A♭
A♭	F	B♭ E♭ A♭ D♭
D♭	B♭	B♭ E♭ A♭ D♭ G♭
G♭	E♭	B♭ E♭ A♭ D♭ G♭ C♭
C♭	A♭	B♭ E♭ A♭ D♭ G♭ C♭ F♭

Functional Words

Musicians use specific words to describe each scale degree's function. The first scale degree is known as the **tonic**. The tonic is the root of the key and the home base that all the notes eventually resolve to.

The second degree of the scale is called the **supertonic**. The prefix super- generally means above or beyond, so one note above the tonic is known as the supertonic.

The third scale degree is known as the **mediant**. It lies halfway between the tonic and the dominant.

We call the fourth scale degree the **subdominant**. It is one degree below the fifth, which we call the **dominant**. However, if you count down from the root (C - B - A - G - F) you will find the fourth scale degree is a fifth below the root. This is the real reason the fourth scale degree is known as the subdominant.

As mentioned, the fifth scale degree is known as the dominant. For about two or three centuries, music was defined by the resolution of the dominant chord to the tonic chord. This resolution is called a perfect cadence and provides a firm sense of completion and finality.

The sixth scale degree is called the **submediant**. The sixth scale degree is a third below the root, similar to the fourth scale degree which is a fifth below the root. For this reason, we call the sixth scale degree the submediant.

Finally, we call the seventh scale degree the **leading tone** or the **subtonic**. We use the term leading tone when the seventh scale degree is **one half step** below the root. This note has a strong pull toward the root. It wants to resolve, and composers will delay this resolution to increase tension in the music.

When the seventh scale degree is **one whole step** below the root, we call it the **subtonic**. We call it the subtonic because it is an interval of a second below the tonic, just as the second scale degree is an interval of a second above the tonic, hence the name supertonic.

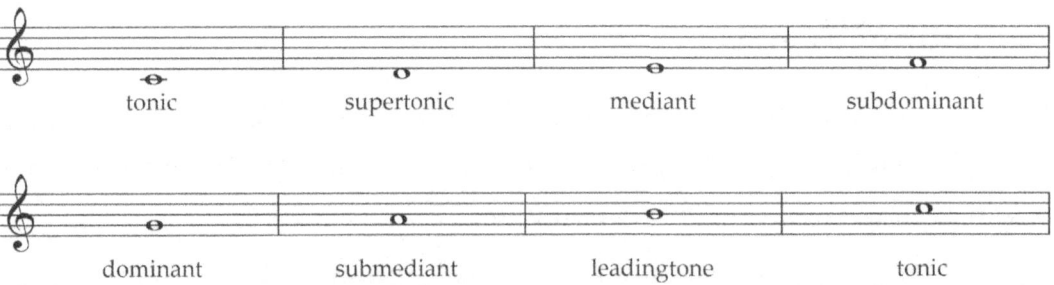

These terms are useful to know, mainly so that you understand them if someone uses them to communicate ideas. You will frequently use the scale degree names to communicate chord progressions and melodic shapes to other musicians. Used in a wide range of contexts, scale degree names are highly beneficial to know and understand!

So, bringing along the concept of scale degrees, our music theory vocabulary extends even further. See the below table for its application to the C Major scale, although it could apply to any scale:

Note	Scale Degree
C	1st degree of the scale is the **tonic**
D	2nd degree of the scale is the **supertonic**
E	3rd degree of the scale is the **mediant**
F	4th degree of the scale is the **subdominant**
G	5th degree of the scale is the **dominant**
A	6th degree of the scale is the **submediant**
B	7th degree of the scale is the **leading tone**

Learning to Use Solfege

In addition to the scale degrees, there is another tool you can use to hear better and understand the relationships between the tones inside a scale. This tool is called *solfege*, a syllabic system used to memorize pitches in relation to one another.

You may have learned some basics of *solfege* in your elementary school music classes or remember the song *"do a deer, a female deer, re a drop of golden sun"* from the movie musical *The Sound of Music*. *"Do"* and *"re"* are solfege syllables.

Check out the *solfege* syllables for the C Major scale written below the staff:

Here's the pronunciation of the *solfege* syllables. Solfege is very important for ear and voice training in music.

C -	**Do** pronounced as "doe"
D -	**Re** pronounced as "ray"
E -	**Mi** pronounced as "me"
F -	**Fa** pronounced as "fah"
G -	**Sol** pronounced as 'so"
A -	**La** pronounced as "lah"
B -	**Ti** pronounced as "tea"
C -	**Do** pronounced as "doe"

Using the *solfege* syllables is a great way to train your ears to hear the pitch relationships between the notes of the major scale. It is also a great way to build your skills of relative pitch, which will help you hear and understand music more deeply.

Solfege can apply to any major scale; hence the *Do* solfege sound, which is the first scale degree or tonic, could also be the F note in an F Major scale or the A♭ in an A♭ Major scale.

A solfege system also exists for the chromatic scale (all 12 notes), which comprise the mentioned seven terms plus an additional five. This may be useful if you're doing voice training.

Of course, learning and using *solfege* is only partially necessary and not often used by musicians in the same way as scale degrees. However, it is still a useful tool to have in your box.

Practice Time

Use these questions and exercises to help practice your skills!

Chapter 4 Questions

1. What is a scale?

2. What is the major scale? What is the interval pattern of the major scale? How do we spell the C Major scale?

3. What is the interval pattern for the natural minor scale?

4. Briefly describe the concept of relative minor/relative major.

5. What are scale degrees? What purpose do scale degrees serve in understanding music theory?

6. On which scale degree is the relative minor of any major key found? On which scale degree is the relative major of any minor key found?

7. What are the functional names of the different scale degrees? What do we call the third degree of the scale? What about the sixth degree? What is the name for the root of the scale?

8. What is *solfege* and what purpose does it serve? In the C Major scale, which tone corresponds to *do* and which tone corresponds to *sol*?

Chapter 4 Exercises

1. Practice spelling the major scale from the following root notes. Tip: the major scale follows the interval pattern: *whole step, whole step, half-step, whole step, whole step, whole step, half-step.*

2. Challenge exercise! Add sharps or flats to turn the following scale into the major scale:

3. Notate the natural minor scale from the following roots:

4. Identify the relative minor in the following major scales. Then, re-notate the corresponding natural minor scale:

Conclusion

In Chapter 4, we broke into the world of **scales**. Remember that scales are simple groups of pitches organized in a sequence based on a particular **interval** pattern. An interval is simply the distance between two notes. We measure intervals in basic units called **half-steps** and **whole steps.** Two half-steps equal one whole step.

The main types of scales are major and minor.

The **major scale** is one of the most common scales in music. It consists of seven notes following the interval pattern of half-steps and whole steps:

Next, we used half-steps and whole steps to build the C Major scale. Think of the C Major scale as a neutral starting place for music theory work. It is a simple scale because it contains all the natural notes from C - C and can easily be played using just the white keys on a piano.

We learned the interval pattern for the C Major scale is whole step, whole step, half-step, whole step, whole step, whole step, half-step. This means that the C

Major scale is spelled C - D - E - F - G - A - B - C. All twelve major scales follow this identical interval pattern of half-steps and whole steps.

The **minor scale** also consists of seven notes with a unique interval pattern between them. There are three types of minor scales, natural, harmonic, and melodic. Unlike major scales, the minor scale sounds sad, darker, solemn, or ominous. This is due to the minor third interval between the 1st and 3rd degrees of the scale.

Other scales explained were the pentatonic, which is a 5-note scale, the chromatic consisting of only half-step intervals, and the whole tone consisting of only whole step intervals.

After that, we built on our knowledge of the major scale and identified the **scale degrees** for each tone. Scale degrees are an extremely useful tool. Essentially, each tone of the scale has a numeral associated with it. The numerals delineate the tone's role in the hierarchy of notes inside the scale. Scale degrees also allow us to communicate musical information in a generic sense and then apply that information to multiple keys.

Musicians use specific words to describe each scale degree's function. The functional names of the scale are *tonic, supertonic, mediant, subdominant, dominant, submediant*, and *subtonic* or *leading tone*. The **tonic** is the key's root and the home base that all the notes eventually resolve to.

Finally, we briefly touched on the concept of ***solfege***, a more antiquated tool that you can use to hear the relationships between pitches in a scale.

In the next chapter, we will explore how we use the major scale to build chords. When you are ready, dive in!

5
Exploring Harmony through Building Chords

Keywords: chords, harmony, chord progression, triads, major triad, major third, perfect fifth, minor triad, minor third, diminished triad, diminished fifth, chord, scale

The Basics of Chords

Chords and **harmony** are integral and wonderful components of music. Think of chords as analogous to color. Melodies are like lines, rhythm helps give form and structure like a skeleton, and chords bring color, shading, and gradient to music. All three of these elements combine to create beautiful music.

Chords are the harmonious building blocks of music. They evoke emotion and provide the foundation for creating many melodies. They can also stand on their own, as in **chord progressions**. Learning how chords are constructed and how different chords interact with each other and with melodies and rhythm is a fundamental aspect of music theory.

In essence, a chord happens anytime we **play two or more notes simultaneously**. The most basic example of chords is two voices singing together. In fact, this is a primary source of chords. We didn't always have chords in the way we think about them today. The modern concept of chords only really emerged during the Renaissance period, with the rise of instrumental and vocal music in social settings.

Different Types of Chords

While the world of chords is as open as you could imagine, there are a handful of basic patterns and shapes that every beginning music theorist should understand how to build and use. We can categorize chords in several different ways, and you can create chords from any combination of the twelve notes.

At their foundation, all chords are built from a fundamental pitch called the **root**. From there, we can take any number of twists and turns to build rich and interesting harmonies that move the emotions of our listeners in whichever way we desire.

The most basic harmony used in modern music is the **triad**. A triad is simply a **three-note chord**. Any word with the prefix tri- refers to a group of three, like a triangle or triceratops.

Triads are everywhere in music. They sound great, are easy to work with, have a wide range of applications, and can be varied quite a bit. The four basic families of triads are: major, minor, diminished, and augmented.

Major Triads

Major triads are generally the first type of triads that beginners learn. Major triads sound bright, happy, and light and are found everywhere in music.

The formula for the major triad is quite simple. Beginning with the root, count up a **major third** (four half-steps), followed by a **minor third** (three half-steps). That's it. A major triad is simply a major third followed by a minor third.

Put another way, the major chord consists of the root, a major third and a perfect fifth. A perfect fifth is seven half-steps from the root.

Try now to build a C Major triad. Beginning with the root C, count up four half-steps (C - C♯ - D - D♯ - E), then up three half-steps (E - F - F♯ - G). This means a C Major triad is spelled C - E - G. Did you notice that G is a perfect fifth above the C?

Using our scale degree numbering learned in the previous chapter, the formula for any major triad will always be 1 - 3 - 5.

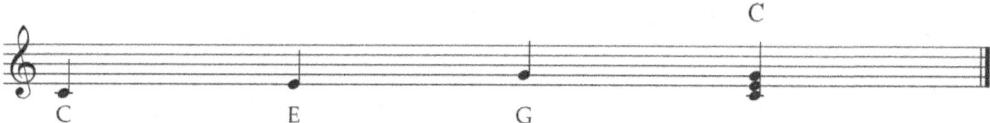

Here is a list of some basic major triads:

D Major: D - F♯ - A

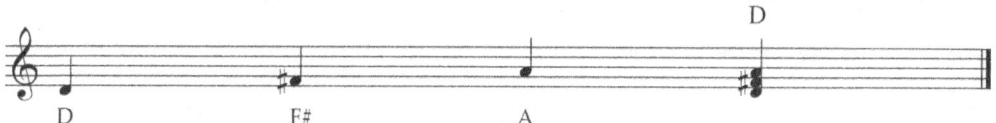

E Major: E - G♯ - B

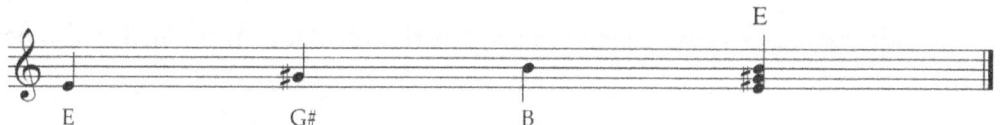

F Major: F - A - C

G Major: G - B - D

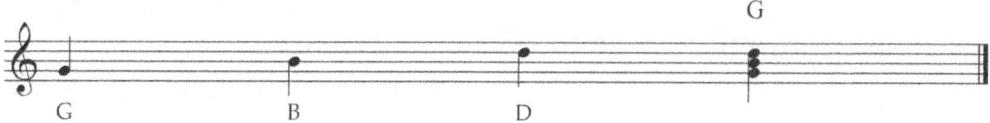

A Major: A - C♯ - E

B Major: B - D♯ - F♯

Minor Triads

Minor triads lend a darker shade or hue to our music. They provide a great counterpoint to major triads and can imbue your music with greater emotional depth. From a theoretical view, minor triads are the inverse of major triads.

To build a minor triad, begin with the root. Count up a **minor third** (three semitones), then count up a **major third** (four half-steps). A minor triad comprises a minor third, followed by a major third – the inverse of a major triad.

Put another way, the minor chord consists of the root, a minor third and a perfect fifth.

Try using this information to build a few minor triads. Start with F minor. Beginning with the root F, count up three half-steps (F - G♭ - G - A♭), then up four half-steps (A♭ - A - B♭ - B - C). This means that a F minor triad is spelled F - A♭ - C.

Try one more, this time C minor. Starting with the root C, count up three half-steps (C - D♭ - D - E♭), followed by four half-steps (E♭ - E - F - G♭ - G). This means that a C minor triad is spelled C - E♭ - G.

Now, compare the spelling of the C Major triad to that of the C minor triad. The C Major triad is spelled C - E - G, while the C minor triad is spelled C -

Eb - G. If the formula for any major triad is 1 - 3 - 5, and the only difference between C Major and C minor is a lowered third scale degree, this means the formula for any minor triad will be 1 - b3 - 5.

Here is a list of some common minor triads:

C minor: C - Eb - G

D minor: D - F - A

E minor: E - G - B

F minor: F - Ab - C

G minor: G - Bb - D

A minor: A - C - E

B minor: B - D - F♯

Diminished Triads

Diminished triads are an enigmatic and often misunderstood sound. They sound more dissonant than minor triads and find their place best in suspenseful or tense passages.

A diminished triad comprises **two minor thirds** stacked on top of one another. To build the diminished triad, start with the root and count up a minor third (three half-steps), followed by another minor third. That's it.

Try building a diminished triad from B. Beginning with B, count up three half-steps (B - C - D♭ - D), followed by another three half-steps (D - E♭ - E - F). The B diminished triad is spelled B - D - F.

Now try to build the diminished triad from C, so we can compare it to our other triads and derive a formula. Beginning with C, count up a minor third (C - D♭ - D - E♭), followed by another minor third (E♭ - E - F - G♭). The C diminished triad is spelled C - E♭ - G♭.

Comparing this to the formula for a minor triad (1 - ♭3 - 5), we find that the diminished triad has a flat fifth scale degree compared to the minor triad. We call this fifth a **diminished fifth**, unlike the **perfect fifth** found in the major and minor triads. This means the formula for any diminished triad will be 1 - ♭3 - ♭5.

Here is a list of some common diminished triads:

C diminished: C - E♭ - G♭

D diminished: D - F - A♭

E diminished: E - G - B♭

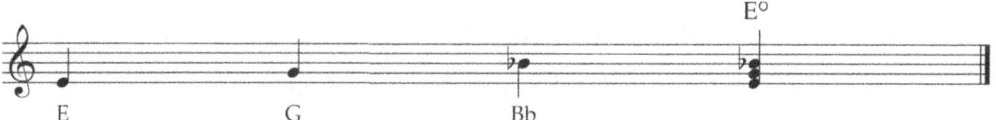

F diminished: F - A♭ - C♭

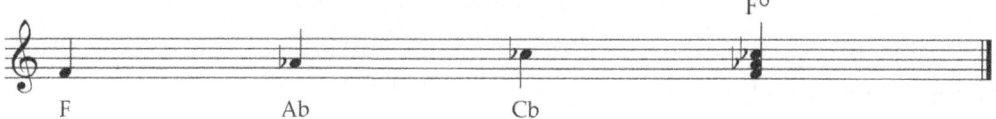

G diminished: G - B♭ - D♭

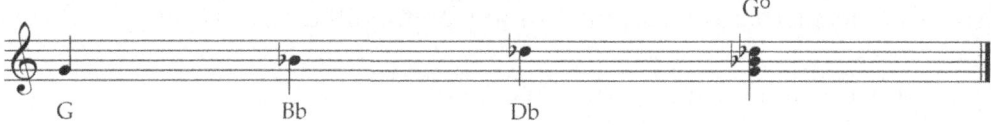

A diminished: A - C - E♭

B diminished: B - D - F

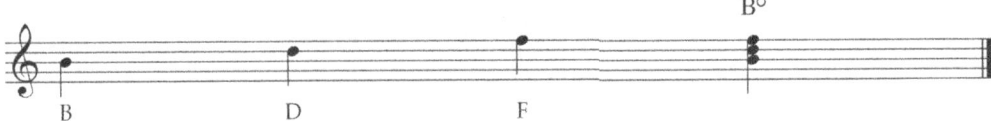

Augmented Triads

The final family of triads we will dive into here is augmented triads. Augmented triads are a variation of major triads and have an ethereal and otherworldly sound. Similar to the diminished triad, the augmented chord is symmetrical. It is built from the combination of two major thirds.

To build the augmented triad, start with the root and count up a major third (four half-steps), followed by another major third. Simple. If you start with the root D, count up a major third (D - D♯ - E - F - F♯), followed by another major third (F♯ - G - G♯ - A - A♯). This means D augmented triad is spelled D - F♯ - A♯.

Now try building a C augmented triad so we can compare it to our C Major triad. Begin with C and count up a major third (C - C♯ - D - D♯ - E), followed by another major third (E - F - F♯ - G - G♯). This means that a C augmented triad is spelled C - E - G♯.

When we compare this with the C major triad (C - E - G), we find that the C augmented triad has a raised fifth scale degree, also known as the **augmented fifth**. This means that the formula for any augmented triad will be 1 - 3 - ♯5.

Here is a list of some basic augmented triads:

C augmented: C - E - G♯

D augmented: D - F♯ - A♯

E augmented: E - G♯ - B♯

F augmented: F - A - C♯

G augmented: G - B - D♯

A augmented: A - C♯ - E♯

B augmented: B - D♯ - F𝄪

Building a Chord Scale

Now that we understand the four basic families of triads, let's combine them into a **chord scale**. A chord scale happens when we build chords on the tones of a scale. The chord scale we will analyze here is built on the major scale.

Remember, the C Major scale is spelled C - D - E - F - G - A - B - C. Building the C Major chord scale is quite simple. All we need to do is determine which type of triad is built naturally from each tone of the scale.

We can do this by starting with a root note and counting up by thirds through the scale, which is equal to skipping every other tone. For example, remember that the C Major triad is spelled C - E - G. Start with C, skip up a note in the scale to E, and skip up one more to G.

Building triads using the scale of C major looks like this:

C - E – G which forms a Major Triad
D – F – A which forms a Minor Triad
E - G – B which forms a Minor Triad
F - A – C which forms a Major Triad
G - B – D which forms a Major Triad
A - C – E which forms a Minor Triad
B - D – F which forms a Diminished Triad

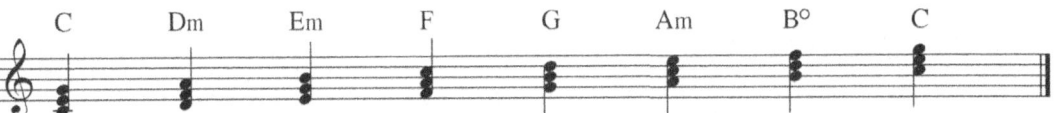

This means that the formula for any major chord scale is:

Major - Minor - Minor - Major - Major - Minor - Diminished

Every major scale follows this pattern. It is extremely useful to memorize and practice this pattern, as it will unlock the doors to understanding how chords work in all twelve keys.

The letters C, Dm and Em and so forth are written above the staff. The diminished chord is an 'o' next to the letter name. These are **chord symbols** and tell which chords to play. Some written music shows only these symbols without a staff. Stay on your music journey long enough, and soon you be able to read them too without a staff.

Adding in Roman Numerals

Remember from the previous chapter that each note in a scale has a particular number associated with it. We call these numbers scale degrees. We can take this concept a step further with chords by using Roman numerals to distinguish each chord's role and function in the scale.

The first chord of any major key is called the I chord. The second chord is labeled 'ii.' The third chord is labeled 'iii.' The fourth chord is labeled 'IV.' The fifth chord is labeled 'V.' The sixth chord is labeled 'vi.' And the seventh chord is labeled 'vii.'

Chords with a **capital** Roman numeral such, as I, IV, and V are **major chords**. Chords with a **lower-case** Roman numeral such as ii, iii, vi, and vii are **minor or diminished chords**. Here is what this pattern looks like on the staff:

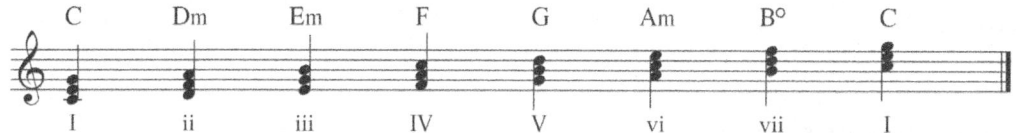

Chord Progression

Understanding and manipulating these Roman numerals will allow you to communicate chord progressions to other musicians more easily. A **chord progression** is playing one chord to the next, to the next, etc. This progression gives a sense of forward movement and moments of emotional tension, all ingredients that make a great song!

Instead of describing a particular chord progression as C Major - D minor - F Major, you can say I - ii - IV. This allows you to move the chord progression into any key you desire because every major scale follows this same pattern of chord qualities.

Let's practice using these Roman numerals to describe chord progressions in the key of C Major. Let's start with a simple chord progression: C Major - F Major - G Major. C major is the I chord, F major is the IV chord, and G major is the V chord. This means we can call this chord progression 'I - IV - V.' The I - IV - V chord progression is one of the most common chord progressions in Western music.

What about the chord progression F Major - G Major - D minor - C Major? F Major is the IV chord, G Major is the V chord, D minor is the ii chord, and C Major is the I chord. So the Roman numerals for this chord progression are 'IV - V - ii - I.' Make sense?

Let's try a few more. What about the chord progression E minor - A minor - D minor - G Major - C Major? E minor is the iii chord, A minor is the vi chord, D minor is the ii chord, G Major is the V chord, and C Major is the I chord. This means the Roman numerals for this chord progression are iii - vi - ii - V - I. Again, this is another extremely common progression you often hear in music.

Chord Inversion

So far, we've seen the root note as the lowest, the third in the middle, and the fifth on the top. This doesn't have to always be this way. It's perfectly acceptable for the chords to be played in a different order so that the root isn't the lowest note. The same applies to the middle note and the third.

Where the third is placed as the lowest note, we call this the **first inversion**. Using the C Major chord C - E - G, this would be played E - G - C. Where the fifth of the chord is placed at the bottom, followed by the root and the third to look like G - C - E, this is called the **second inversion**.

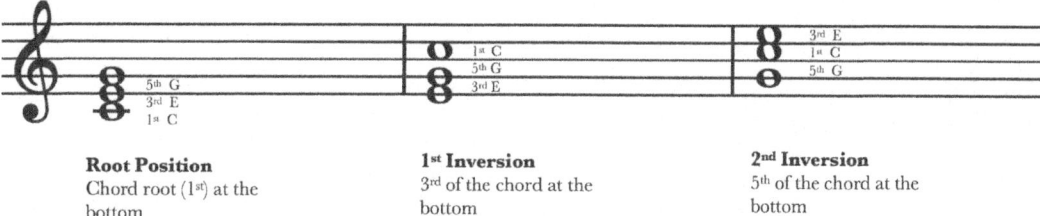

Root Position
Chord root (1st) at the bottom

1st Inversion
3rd of the chord at the bottom

2nd Inversion
5th of the chord at the bottom

Chord inversions give music an altogether different avenue of expression, allowing the same group of notes to sound in entirely new ways. This also applies to placement of notes on the bass clef.

Practice Time!

Use these questions and exercises to help practice your skills!

Chapter 5 Questions

1. How many notes does it take to make a chord?

2. What is the most common type of chord, and how many notes does it have?

3. What are the four main families of triads?

4. What is the interval structure of a major triad? What about a minor triad? What is so interesting about the relationship between major and minor triads?

5. What is a chord scale?

6. How do the Roman numerals we learned from the chord scale compare to the scale degree numbers we learned in Chapter 4?

Chapter 5 Exercises

1. Build major triads from the following roots:

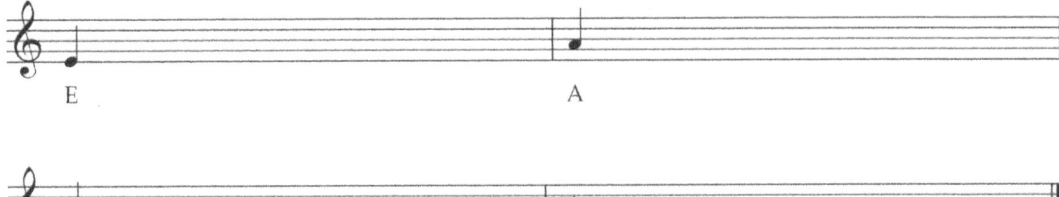

2. Build minor triads from the following roots:

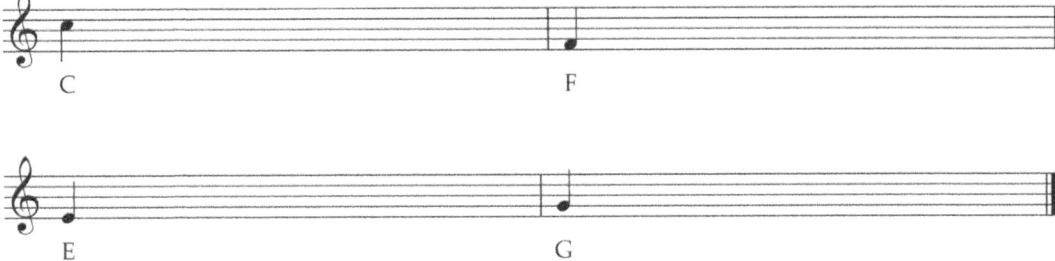

3. Build diminished triads from the following roots:

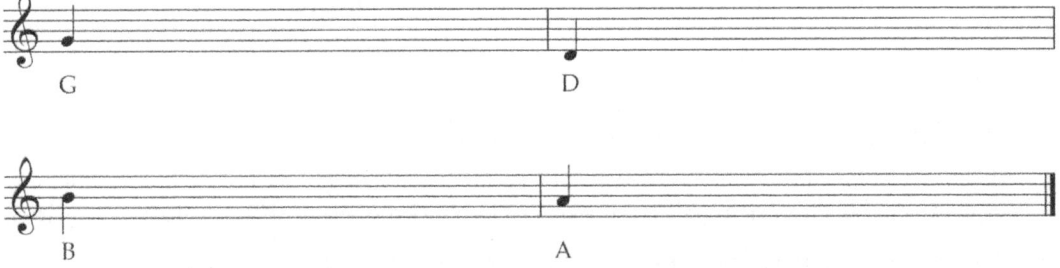

4. Turn the following minor triads into major triads:

5. Notate the following chord progressions in the key of C major using the following Roman numerals:

(a) vi - ii - V - I

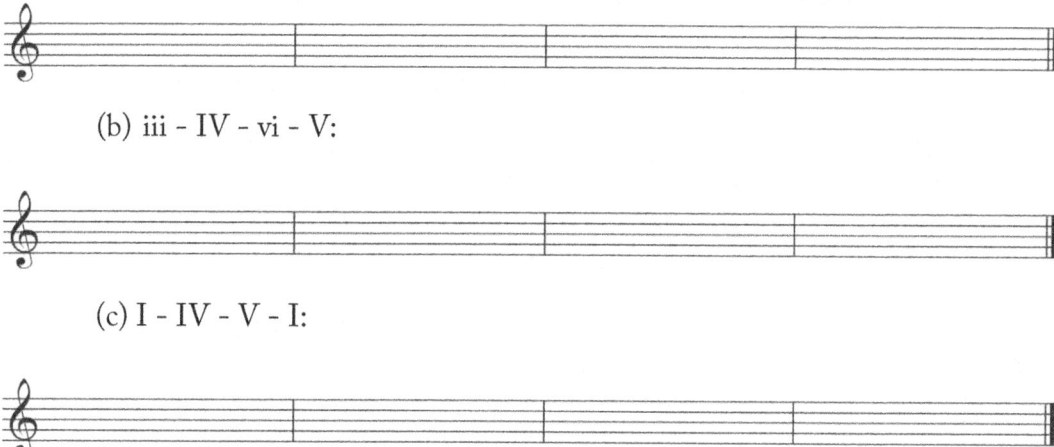

(b) iii - IV - vi - V:

(c) I - IV - V - I:

Conclusion

Chords help provide color, gradient, and shade to music. They help propel music forward, provide a sense of resolution, and help us deeply affect listeners' emotions.

At their most basic, chords are the combination of two or more notes **played simultaneously**. Our modern concept of chords emerged out of vocal music from the monasteries of the Renaissance period.

The most common type of chord is the **triad**. There are four main families of triads: **major, minor, diminished**, and **augmented**. If you want to understand their secrets, you have to spend time playing and thinking about their formulas. There are no shortcuts in music.

Lastly, we explored the concept of the **chord scale** and some Roman numerals. A chord scale is simply a collection of chords built from the notes of a scale. The pattern of chord qualities for any major chord scale is major, minor, minor, major, major, minor, diminished. Every major scale follows this pattern and it will be to your benefit to study and understand it in all twelve keys.

We then applied our knowledge of scale degrees to the chord scale and added in the Roman numerals to help distinguish the role and function of each chord in the chord scale. Learning to master Roman numerals will allow you to easily translate **chord progressions** from one key to another and will allow you to see larger patterns in how music works!

6
Key Signatures & Circle of Fifths

Keywords: key signature, Circle of Fifths, relative major, relative minor

Key Signatures: How Pitches are Organized

Just as we learned in Chapter 2 that we can organize rhythms using a time signature, so too can we organize pitches using a tool called a **key signature**.

In music, a 'key' is essentially a group of pitches organized in a hierarchical manner from a particular root note. The root note is always the name of the key. The root of the key signature carries a certain tonal gravity that draws the other pitches back to it.

Hierarchical manner? Yes, the notes in a particular key signature form a scale so that the music played are all the notes from that scale.

The word "scale" comes from the Italian word "scala" which means "ladder".

Pitches or music notes in a scale move higher or lower, like climbing up or down a ladder.

And we know that the distance from one climb to another, whether up or down, is called an interval.

We know there are 12 distinct pitches, but when we hear music with a pleasing musical tonality, not all 12 pitches are used. In a harmonious composition, only about seven (7) in a specific range are utilized.

Seven notes, sound familiar? Yes, the seven (7) notes correspond to a specific scale, whether C Major, A Major, D Minor, and so on.

If a piece is written as we say, in the key of C Major, it will contain only the notes from that scale. The same with the key of B-flat Major or E minor (with a few exceptions depending on harmony and composition).

Thus, in its simplest, a key signature tells us what seven (7) notes can be played for that piece of music. This is true for the most part in musical genres like classical, pop, rock, or blues music, where the notes played will be from that scale. Jazz, on the other hand, is a bit more complicated, with frequent changeovers into other scales and hence different notes being played.

It also tells us what chords are available for a piece of music, as the chords will be built on the seven (7) available notes. Key signatures also tell us whether a piece has a major or minor key tonality.

Learning to understand how keys work will allow you to learn music faster and understand the chords and scales present in the music so that you can perform and improvise with the music.

Why Different Music Keys?

There are a few answers to this. When music is composed, whether for voice (singing) or a specific instrument, a composer must be aware of what range of pitches that voice or instrument can comfortably perform in.

Some will tell you that a particular key evokes a specific feeling or emotion, like hopeful, melancholic or victorious.

Music can connect to our unconscious and bring out emotions that we are unaware of or understand but still feel. Key signatures do this, as do chord progressions and the application of principles related to harmony and rhythm.

In the 1800s, a musician named Christian Schubard wrote a book ascribing an emotion to what he thought a particular key evoked. It's all very subjective, though not entirely to be disregarded. For example, he described the key of B-flat as "*...cheerful love, a clear conscience, hope, aspiration for a better world*" or C-major described as "*...completely pure. Its character is innocence, simplicity, naïvety, children's talk.*"

When you get to the required level on your musical journey, play around with different keys and come to your own conclusions about what a particular key feels like.

Where to Find the Key Signature?

How do we recognize the key in a piece of music? Well, the same way as other visual music markings such as notes and time signatures. The key signature is a marking shown on the staff in the form of either **sharps or flats** right up front between the clef and time signature. It's a small musical marking that conveys a huge amount of information.

♯	Sharp
♭	Flat

Key signature musical markings

Below is an example of a D-Major key signature with two sharps, namely F-sharp and C-sharp. The key signature is shown by placing two sharp symbols **on the line or space where they reside on the staff.** This means that when you read an F or C note, it must be played as F-sharp and C sharp.

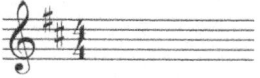

This must be done throughout the music piece unless notated otherwise. The presence of a natural symbol (♮) next to a note in a piece of music will cancel out the sharp or flat for a particular note.

Look at the example below showing B-flat major, which has two flats namely, B-flat and E-flat. Whenever there's a B or E note in the piece, it must be played as B-flat and E-flat.

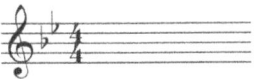

If you see sharps or flats in the key signature, they will not be notated in the music. For example, in the key of G major, which has one sharp F♯, you will not see F♯ notated every time because the F♯ is already in the key signature. You will need to learn to read it automatically. It looks like this:

The only time you will see sharps or flats marked again is if one of the notes has been marked as natural (♮), meaning the sharp or flat has been canceled out like this:

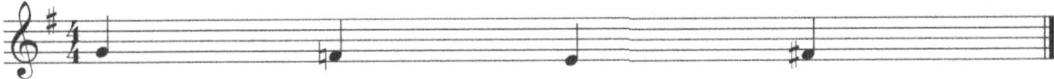

There is one key that has no sharps or flats, namely C-Major hence a piece written in C-Major will have no sharps or flats shown on the staff, as shown below.

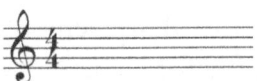

The Circle of Fifths

There is a method to help remember which sharps or flats belong in a key signature. It's called the Circle of Fifths and, as the name hints, shows the addition of a sharp or flat for **every interval of a perfect fifth you move up or down** (clockwise or counterclockwise). Many aspiring musicians keep this circle on hand for easy reference.

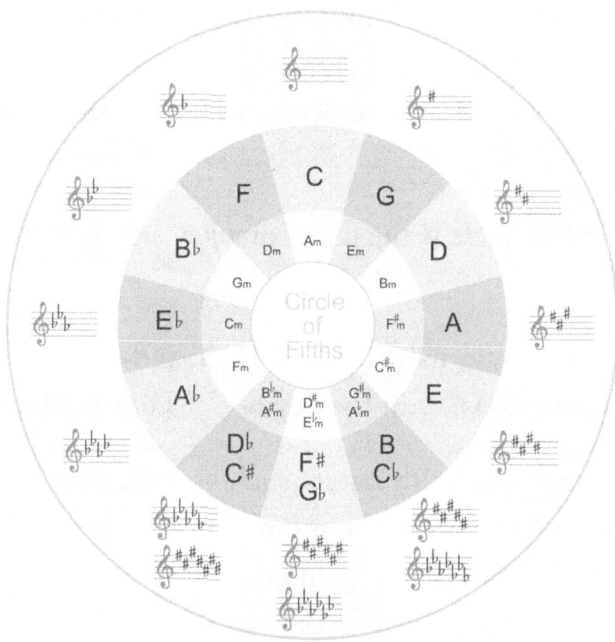

The Circle of Fifths

The Circle of Fifths organizes all twelve pitches a perfect fifth (seven half-steps) apart from one another, starting with C at the 12 o'clock position and moving **clockwise.**

Using the musical alphabet in ascending order, the interval distance from C to G is a perfect fifth, the same with D to A, A to E, E to B and B to F♯ and F♯ to C♯. Continue this pattern around the circle and you'll end up right back to the top C.

In moving clockwise, we see an additional sharp (♯) added for every interval change of a perfect fifth.

We could also move in a counterclockwise direction starting at C. Using the musical alphabet in descending order, the interval distance C to F is a perfect fifth, the same with F to B♭, and so on.

Moving counterclockwise on the left side of the circle, we see an additional flat (♭) added for every interval change of a perfect fifth.

The progression of fifths is likewise mirrored in the addition of either a sharp or flat. This means, each new key adds a flat or a sharp that is a fifth above the sharp or flat before that. Using the progression from G Major (1 sharp = F♯) to D Major (2 sharps = F♯ + C♯), the interval distance of the sharps F♯ and C♯ is a perfect fifth.

Each letter name in the circle is the name of a key signature with its respective number of sharps or flats.

The letters in the outer circle, namely C, G, D, A, and so on, are the major keys. We express key signatures as "…in the key of C Major, or the G Major key."

You'll notice a second circle with letters such as Am, Em, Bm. The lowercase "m" stands for minor and refers to the minor key of that pitch. We express this as "… in the key of A-minor or the E-minor key."

These keys are also the relative minor of the major keys hence their position placed alongside the major key within a segment. Reading the segment for C Major, we see that A-minor is the relative minor key of C Major. Cast your eyes to G Major, and you'll find E-minor is the relative minor key of G Major. Likewise, B-minor is the relative minor of D Major, and so on.

From Chapter 4 you'll remember that the relative major and minor keys contain the exact same pitches. This is why they're shown next to each other in the Circle of Fifths.

The Circle of Fifths is primarily important because it helps us organize the **sequence of key signatures.** This sequence is useful in chord progressions from one key to another (called modulation) and being able to do so in a harmonious tonal manner. It is also useful for composing your own music or transposing music into a different key.

The Major and Relative Minor Keys with Sharps (♯)

Here are the major keys with their relative minor key. Starting at C, each key moves clockwise up an interval of a perfect fifth to the next one with one sharp added to create a new key. In Chapter 4, we learned that the relative minor key begins on the sixth scale degree of the major scale.

C Major, which has zero sharps and zero flats. The relative minor is the key of **A minor.**

G Major contains one sharp: F♯. The relative minor is the key of **E minor**

D Major contains two sharps: F♯ and C♯. The relative minor is the key of **B minor**

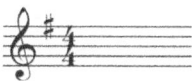

A Major contains three sharps: F♯, C♯, and G♯. The relative minor is the key of **F-sharp minor**

E Major key contains four sharps: F♯, C♯, G♯, and D♯. The relative minor is the key of **C-sharp minor.**

B Major key contains five sharps: F♯, C♯, G♯, D♯, and A♯. The relative minor is the key of **G-sharp minor.**

F-sharp Major key contains six sharps: F♯, C♯, G♯, D♯, A♯, and E♯. The relative minor is the key of **D-sharp minor.**

C-sharp Major contains seven sharps: F♯, C♯, G♯, D♯, A♯, E♯, and B♯. Every note is sharp in the key of C-sharp major. The relative minor is the key of **A-sharp minor**.

The Major and Relative Minor Keys with Flats (♭)

Here we add a flat for every interval of a perfect fifth in a counterclockwise direction on the circle. Again, we'll start with C at 12 o'clock position. From C, the pattern of steps counterclockwise by an interval of a perfect fifth is C - F - B♭ - E♭ - A♭ - D♭ - G♭ - C♭.

C Major, which has zero sharps and zero flats. The relative minor is the key of **A minor**.

F Major contains one flat: B♭ The relative minor is the key of **D minor.**

B-flat Major contains two flats: B♭ and E♭. The relative minor is **G minor.**

E-flat Major contains three flats: B♭, E♭ and A♭. The relative minor is **C minor.**

A-flat Major contains four flats: B♭, E♭, A♭ and D♭. The relative minor is **F minor**

D-flat Major contains five flats: B♭, E♭, A♭, D♭ and G♭. The relative minor is **B-flat minor**

G-flat Major contains six flats: B♭, E♭, A♭, D♭, G♭ and C♭. The relative minor is **E-flat minor**

C-flat Major contains seven flats: B♭, E♭, A♭, D♭, G♭, C♭ and F♭. The relative minor is **A-flat minor**

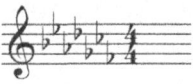

A Few Quick Tricks to Identify the Key Signature

There are a few quick tricks you can use to memorize and easily identify key signatures.

Firstly, you can quickly identify the flat key signatures by looking at the **second-to-last flat positioned on the staff.**

For example, in the key of A♭ Major, four flats are positioned in the following order: B♭, E♭, A♭, and D♭. See below.

The second-to-last flat is A♭, hence this tells us it's the key of A-flat Major.

For key signatures containing sharps, the **last sharp is always a half-step down** from the home key. For example, the key of E Major contains four sharps in the following order: F♯, C♯, G♯, and D♯. See below:

The last sharp is D♯, and it's a half-step down from E, hence the home key is E Major.

A simple way to grasp the various key signatures is to find a free printable of the Circle of Fifths online to keep close by on your musical journey. It's a quick and easy reference; you'll eventually have it memorized with regular study and practice.

Key Signatures & Circle of Fifths

Below is also a table showing the keys signatures with the relative major and minor keys.

Key Signatures								
Major Key	*Sharps or Flats*							*Relative Minor Key*
C Major	-							A minor
G Major	F♯							E minor
D Major	F♯	C♯						B minor
A Major	F♯	C♯	G♯					F-sharp minor
E Major	F♯	C♯	G♯	D♯				C-sharp minor
B Major	F♯	C♯	G♯	D♯	A♯			G-sharp minor
F♯ Major	F♯	C♯	G♯	D♯	A♯	E♯		D-sharp minor
C♯ Major	F♯	C♯	G♯	D♯	A♯	E♯	B♯	A-sharp minor
F Major	B♭							D minor
B♭ Major	B♭	E♭						G minor
E♭ Major	B♭	E♭	A♭					C minor
A♭ Major	B♭	E♭	A♭	D♭				F minor
D♭ Major	B♭	E♭	A♭	D♭	G♭			B-flat minor
G♭ Major	B♭	E♭	A♭	D♭	G♭	C♭		E-flat minor
C♭ Major	B♭	E♭	A♭	D♭	G♭	C♭	F♭	A-flat minor

Major key signatures with corresponding relative minor key signatures

Practice Time!

Use these questions and exercises to help practice your skills!

Chapter 6 Questions

1. What is a key signature, and where do we find it?

2. What do key signatures tell us about a particular piece of music?

3. Which key signature has no sharps and no flats, which has only sharps, and only flats?

4. What is the Circle of Fifths?

5. What important information does the Circle of Fifths give us?

6. How does the progression of sharps and flats around the Circle of Fifths compare to the pitches on the Circle?

Chapter 6 Exercises

1. Practice building the Circle of Fifths:

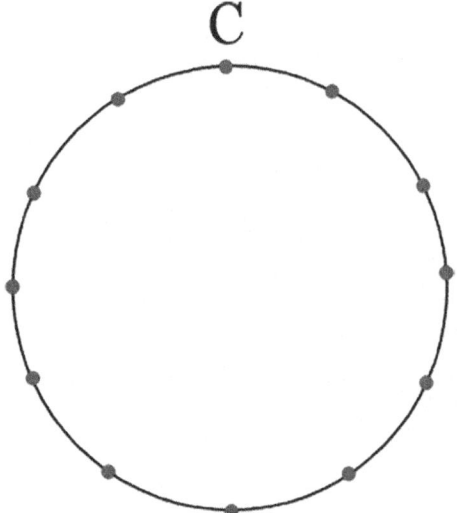

2. Identify the following key signatures:

Conclusion

In music, a key signature is a group of pitches organized in a hierarchical manner from a particular root note in the form of a scale. The root note is always the name of the key. The root of the key signature carries a certain tonal gravity that draws the other pitches back to it.

A key comprises seven (7) notes corresponding to a major or minor scale pattern.

The **Circle of Fifths** is like a musical wheel. It is a logical and cohesive method of organizing all twelve pitches an equal distance of a perfect fifth apart.

The Circle of Fifths also neatly organizes the ascending and descending order of sharp and flat key signatures in a way that is highly logical and easy to understand. Knowing this will help guide which notes to play in a key and its scale chords and progressions to produce pleasing and harmonious music.

Practice building the Circle until you have it memorized. It's a valuable tool to analyze and visualize many relationships in music theory.

7

Exploring the Modes

Keywords: modes, Ionian, Dorian, Phrygian, Lydian, Mixolydian, Aeolian, Locrian

Modes are a deep and fascinating concept. You can spend many hours exploring the modes and constantly finding new and interesting sounds and colors. To many beginners, the modes may seem confusing and mysterious.

Hopefully, after reading through this chapter, however, you will have a solid grasp of the various modes of the major scale, how they are constructed, and how you can use them.

What is a Mode?

In essence, **modes** are scales derived from a parent scale or set of notes. All the modes in one key share the same basic set of pitches. The distinct character of each mode is created by shifting the root or focal point but maintaining the intervallic pattern. It is really quite simple.

Modes existed in ancient Greece before the "major' and 'minor' scales you've learned about already, hence their Greek-sounding names. The seven modes are called Ionian, Dorian, Phrygian, Lydian, Mixolydian, Aeolian and Locrian.

In Chapter 3, we learned the intervallic structure and formula for the major scale. Remember that the C major scale is spelled C - D - E - F - G - A - B - C with a step intervallic pattern of Whole - Whole - Half - Whole - Whole - Whole - Half. There are **seven unique pitches** in this scale before we start again on C.

To create the various modes, we use each of these pitches as the root or focal point of the scale and therefore change the overall character and sound of the scale. The scale's character and sound change because the intervallic pattern changes.

Look at the table below and observe the changes in intervallic pattern for each shift in the root or focal point. The pitches remain the same, but a unique interval pattern emerges due to the change in root as starting point of the scale.

Intervallic Pattern

	W	W	H	W	W	W	H	W	W	H	W	W	W
C-Ionian	C	D	E	F	G	A	B	C	D	E	F	G	A	B
D-Dorian		D	E	F	G	A	B	C	D	E	F	G	A	B
E-Phrygian			E	F	G	A	B	C	D	E	F	G	A	B
F-Lydian				F	G	A	B	C	D	E	F	G	A	B
G-Mixolydian					G	A	B	C	D	E	F	G	A	B
A-Aeolian						A	B	C	D	E	F	G	A	B
B-Locrian							B	C	D	E	F	G	A	B

W = Whole Step
H = Half-Step

In modal language, the major scale is called the **Ionian** mode. The Ionian mode is the same thing as the major scale. This means that the C Ionian mode is spelled C - D - E - F - G - A - B - C, just like the major scale with the exact same interval pattern. There is no difference.

Now, if we begin the scale from D while keeping all the pitches the same, we create the **Dorian** mode, the second mode of the major scale. This means that the D Dorian mode (Dorian mode starting on D) is spelled D - E - F - G - A - B - C - D.

The interval pattern changes to Whole - Half - Whole - Whole - Whole - Half – Whole.

These pitches played in this order have a completely **different character and sound** to the C Ionian mode, even though the same pitches are used. By shifting the focal point of the scale, we also **shift the intervallic pattern** of the notes, thereby creating an entirely different sound! Awesome, right?

If we begin the scale from E, we find the **Phrygian** mode, the third mode of the major scale. The E Phrygian mode is spelled E - F - G - A - B - C - D - E.

Starting the scale from F forms the **Lydian** mode. The Lydian mode is the fourth mode of the major scale. The F Lydian mode is spelled F - G - A - B - C - D - E - F.

Beginning the scale with G forms the **Mixolydian** mode. The Mixolydian mode is the fifth mode of the major scale. The G Mixolydian mode is spelled G - A - B - C - D - E - F - G.

If we start the scale from A, we come across the **Aeolian** mode. The Aeolian mode is the sixth mode of the major scale. The A Aeolian mode is spelled A - B - C - D - E - F - G - A. This is the same sequence of pitches as the A natural minor scale. Yes, the A natural minor scale and the A Aeolian mode are the same scale.

Finally, when we begin the scale from B, we hear the mysterious and enigmatic **Locrian** mode. The Locrian mode is the seventh and final mode of the major scale. The B Locrian mode is spelled B - C - D - E - F - G - A - B.

Each of these modes contains the same pitches. What differentiates each mode is **the root or focal point of the scale.** By shifting the root around while keeping the pitch set the same, we create many new worlds of sound and texture.

Why Bother Learning Modes?

Musical modes give you an expanded palette of emotional options beyond the standard major and minor dichotomy of happy or sad. One great realization about experimenting with different modes is that changing modes immediately changes the feeling and flavor of your music.

Changing the mode also allows you to emphasize different notes of the scale. This change in note emphasis is where the differences and the "flavor" of modes lie. Consider trying modes to introduce new tonalities, variety, and vibe into your music. Modes can evoke emotion by sounding dark, bright, happy, sad, tense, heavenly, epic, and many other perceived characteristics.

Modes are so ubiquitous in contemporary music that it is essential to learn them. If you do not, you will lack a particular understanding and depth of knowledge about the possibilities of music. You will also miss out on understanding why certain music elicits a particular emotional response.

The Intervallic Patterns of Modes

So far, we've learned that modes are created by shifting the root or focal point of the scale. We use the same pitches, and as a result, the intervallic pattern between the pitches changes to create a unique sound. Let's explore those intervallic patterns in more detail.

Ionian Mode

The Ionian mode is the first mode of the major scale. As mentioned above, the words Ionian mode and major scale are synonymous.

We are playing or hearing the Ionian mode when we play or hear the major scale. Therefore, the Ionian mode follows the same intervallic structure and formula as the major scale, namely:

Whole - Whole - Half - Whole - Whole - Whole - Half

The formula in scale degrees for the Ionian mode is:

1 - 2 - 3 - 4 - 5 - 6 - 7

Dorian Mode

The Dorian Mode is the second mode of the major scale.

The D Dorian mode is spelled D - E - F - G - A - B - C - D.

Let's take it apart, analyze the intervallic structure, and build a formula for the Dorian mode.

From D to E is one whole step. From E to F is one half-step. From F to G is one whole step. From G to A is one whole step. From A to B is one whole step. From B to C is one half-step. And finally, from C to D is one whole step. This means the intervallic structure of the Dorian mode is:

Whole - Half - Whole - Whole - Whole - Half – Whole

If we compare the notes of D Dorian to the notes of the D major scale (D - E - F♯ - G - A - B - C♯ - D), we realize that we have a flat third degree and a flat seventh degree. This means that the Dorian mode is a minor scale (as it features a flattened third degree) with natural sixth and flat seven scale degrees. This means the formula for the Dorian mode is:

1 - 2 - ♭3 - 4 - 5 - 6 - ♭7

Phrygian Mode

The Phrygian mode is the third mode of the major scale. The E Phrygian mode is spelled E - F - G - A - B - C - D - E.

Following a similar interval analysis as before, we find that the interval structure of the Phrygian mode is:

Half - Whole - Whole - Whole - Half - Whole - Whole

When we compare the notes of the E Phrygian mode to the notes of the E major scale (E - F♯ - G♯ - A - B - C♯ - D♯ - E), we find that the E Phrygian mode has flat second, third, sixth, and seventh scale degrees. This means the formula for the Phrygian mode is:

1 - ♭2 - ♭3 - 4 - 5 - ♭6 - ♭7

The Phrygian mode is a minor scale (as it has a flat third) with flat second, sixth, and seventh scale degrees. It is one shade darker than the natural minor scale, which only features flat third, sixth, and seventh scale degrees.

The half-step between the root and the second note is the defining feature of the Phrygian mode. To create a Phrygian mode, take any minor scale and lower the 2nd scale degree by a half-step. Explore this sound to get a grip on its dark and mysterious character.

Lydian Mode

The Lydian mode is the fourth mode of the major scale. The F Lydian mode is spelled F - G - A - B - C - D - E - F.

The interval structure of the Lydian mode is:

Whole - Whole - Whole - Half - Whole - Whole - Half

To create a Lydian mode, take any major scale and raise the 4th degree by a half-step. For example, the F-Major scale has B♭ as the 4th scale degree. To create a Lydian mode, the 4th scale degree is raised by a half-step and becomes B.

The formula for the Lydian mode is:

1 - 2 - 3 - ♯4 - 5 - 6 - 7

The Lydian mode is often considered brighter and lighter than the Ionian mode. It has an ethereal and otherworldly sound. Because of the raised 4th scale degree, it also has a natural resolution to the 5th scale degree.

Mixolydian Mode

The Mixolydian mode is the fifth mode of the major scale. The G Mixolydian mode is spelled G - A - B - C - D - E - F - G.

The intervallic structure of the Mixolydian mode is:

Whole - Whole - Half - Whole - Whole - Half - Whole

The Mixolydian mode is a major mode with a flat seventh scale degree.

1 - 2 - 3 - 4 - 5 - 6 - ♭7

It has a broader and more open character than the major scale, while retaining the bright nature of major tonality. It is commonly used in folk, rock, and jazz music.

Aeolian Mode

The Aeolian mode is the sixth mode of the major scale. The A Aeolian mode is spelled A - B - C - D - E - F - G - A.

The intervallic structure of the Mixolydian mode is:

Whole - Half - Whole - Whole - Half - Whole - Whole

The Aeolian mode is the same as the natural minor scale. To create an Aeolian mode, take any major scale and lower the 3rd, 6th, and 7th scale degrees. The formula for the Aeolian mode is:

1 - 2 - ♭3 - 4 - 5 - ♭6 - ♭7

Locrian Mode

The seventh and final mode of the major scale is called the Locrian mode. The Locrian mode is more obscure and used less frequently, but it is a beautiful and enigmatic scale that deserves a proper understanding and exploration.

The B Locrian mode is spelled B - C - D - E - F - G - A - B.

The intervallic structure of the Locrian mode is:

Half - Whole - Whole - Half - Whole - Whole - Whole

The Locrian mode is considered the darkest sounding of all the modes, and it is the home of the diminished chord. You don't hear the Locrian mode used extremely often, but it is a fascinating scale worth your time and investigation.

To create a Locrian mode, take any minor scale and lower the 2nd and 5th scale degree.

$$1 - \flat2 - \flat3 - 4 - \flat5 - \flat6 - \flat7$$

The Modes on a Spectrum

Within one key, the seven modes of the major scale all contain the same pitches. What differentiates the seven modes is which note we place as the root or focal point of the scale. Using a different root creates a different mood and flavor. These moods can be organized on a spectrum from darker to lighter like this:

Darker ← → **Lighter**
Locrian - Phrygian - Aeolian - Dorian - Mixolydian - Ionian - Lydian

Modes on a spectrum dark to light

The Locrian mode is generally considered the "darkest" sounding mode because of its flat second, third, fifth, sixth, and seventh scale degrees. On the other side of the spectrum is the brightest-sounding Lydian mode with its raised forth scale degree,

When we talk about what key a piece of music is in, we express the tonality (or tone/pitch) and the modality (the type of scale on that pitch), so that, for example 'B-minor' tells us the tonic is 'B' and the modality is 'minor'. Similarly, we can say "D Lydian" meaning the tonic is 'D' based on the scale of 'Lydian'.

Tips to Create a Mode

There are three 'major' modes containing a major third and four 'minor' modes containing a minor third. This means the intervallic pattern from the 1st to 3rd degree is either a major or minor third.

Lydian, Ionian, and Mixolydian are "major" modes and Aeolian, Dorian, Phrygian and Locrian are "minor".

In the table below, the intervallic pattern from the 1st to 3rd degree is either a major or minor third. After that, each mode looks a little different, but it's a neat way to remember how the mode will start. The order of the modes is from lighter to darker sounding.

Mode from lighter to darker	Scale Degree						
Major Modes							
Lydian (raise 4th)	1	2	3	♯4	5	6	7
Ionian	1	2	3	4	5	6	7
Mixolydian (lower 7th)	1	2	3	4	5	6	♭7
Minor Modes							
Dorian	1	2	♭3	4	5	6	♭7
Aeolian	1	2	♭3	4	5	♭6	♭7
Phrygian (lower 2nd)	1	♭2	♭3	4	5	♭6	♭7
Locrian (lower 2nd & 5th)	1	♭2	♭3	4	♭5	♭6	♭7

Remember that you can do this with any pitch or tone as focal point. Can you see how a whole repertoire of sounds is possible?

Practice Time!

Use these questions and exercises to help practice your skills!

Chapter 7 Questions

1. What is a mode?

2. How many modes are there? What are their names?

3. Which modes are major modes, and which modes are minor modes? Tip: Remember, major modes have a major third above the root as the third scale degree, and minor modes have a minor third.

4. Each mode has a defining feature. What is the defining feature of the Lydian mode? What defines the Dorian mode? What about the Phrygian mode?

5. Why bother exploring modes?

Chapter 7 Exercises

1. Notate the following modes:

    Tip: Determine the intervallic pattern of the mode and apply to the root note.

Conclusion

In Chapter 7, we looked at the fascinating world of **modes**. Modes offer an expanded palette of tonal colors to choose from and expand the possibilities beyond the basic major/minor binary. We hear them commonly used in pop and jazz music, and film composers often use them to create distinct tonal variety for characters or scenes.

There are seven modes of the major scale, one built on each of the seven pitches of the scale. While each of the modes contains all the same pitches, by shifting the root or focal point of the scale, we change the scale's character and create a unique interval pattern and sound.

In order from lightest to darkest, the seven modes are: Lydian, Ionian, Mixolydian, Dorian, Aeolian, Phrygian and Locrian

Each of the twelve major scales contains all seven of these modes. Learning to build and play with each one will help expand your understanding of music and allow you to compose new and exciting music that you might not have otherwise created.

However, remember to have fun, play with all these concepts, and not get too bogged down in the theoretical side!

8
Exploring Seventh Chords

Keywords: seventh chords, major seventh, dominant seventh, minor seventh, half-diminished, minor seventh flat five, fully diminished seventh, chord extensions, major 9th, major 7th ♯11, dominant 9th, dominant 13th, minor 9th

A Wider World of Harmony

In this chapter, we will explore the rich and colorful world of seventh chords and extensions. This chapter will present more advanced material, so make sure you have a firm grasp of the chord concepts from Chapter 5. You will need those fundamental skills to understand this chapter's materials fully.

What are Seventh Chords?

At a basic level, seventh chords are **four-note chords**. They are basic triads with an added tone: the seventh degree of the scale. Remember from Chapter 5 that all the basic triad families follow some variation on the pattern 1 - 3 - 5. A triad is built from the root, the third degree, and the fifth degree of a scale.

To build a seventh chord, all you need to do is **add the seventh degree** of the scale to your triad to make it 1 - 3 - 5 - 7. It is no more complicated than that however, by simply adding one note, you open a whole new palette of musical color.

The Main Families of Seventh Chords

There are four main families of seventh chords:

- major seventh
- dominant seventh
- minor seventh
- diminished seventh

Each of these different qualities of seventh chord has a particular interval structure and formula. You will find they have a much deeper and richer tonal quality than the basic triads.

Major Seventh Chords

Major seventh chords are the first family of seventh chords we will explore. They sound perhaps more melancholic than a basic major triad, but you should spend time exploring these sounds and building your own associations with them.

The C major seventh chord is spelled C - E - G - B. All we do is take the C major triad (C - E - G) and add the natural seventh scale degree, B. Remember from Chapter 4 that a major triad is the combination of a major third followed by a minor third.

If you count from G to B (G - A♭ - A - B♭ - B), you will find it is equal to four half-steps or a major third. This means that the interval structure of a major seventh chord is a **major third, minor third, then a major third.**

The formula for any major seventh chord will be 1 - 3 - 5 - 7 because all we did was add the natural seventh scale degree to the major triad. Here is a C Major seventh chord notated on the staff:

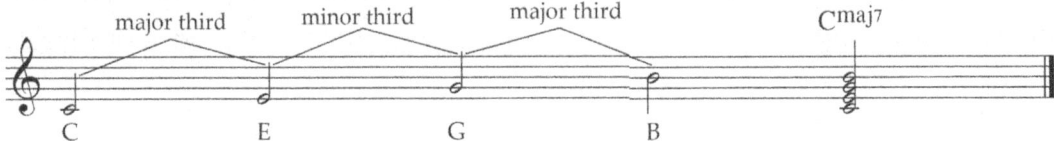

Exploring Seventh Chords

Here is a list of some common major seventh chords:

D Major 7 : D - F♯ - A - C♯

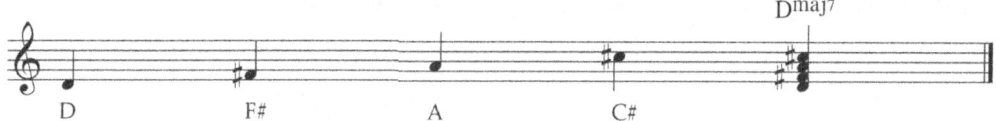

E Major 7 : E - G♯ - B - D♯

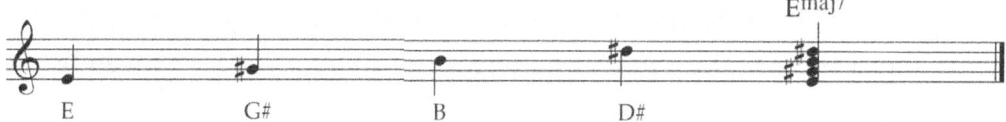

F Major 7 : F - A - C - E

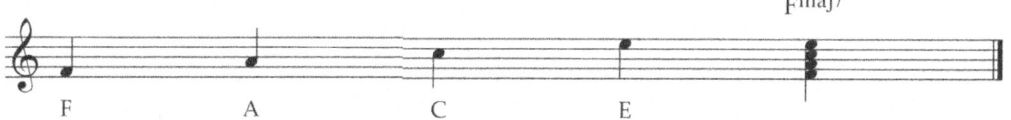

G Major 7 : G - B - D - F♯

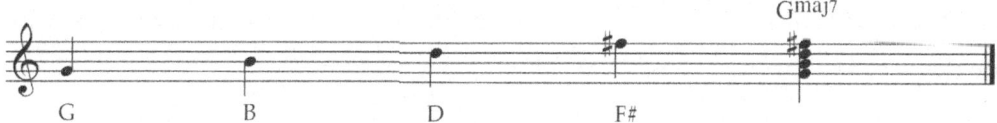

A Major 7 : A - C♯ - E - G♯

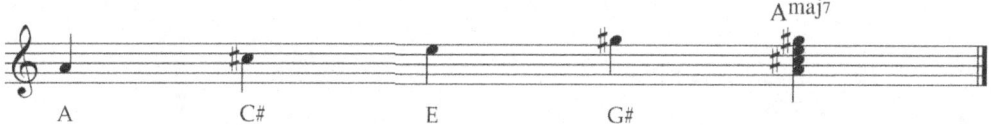

B Major 7 : B - D♯ - F♯ - A♯

Dominant Seventh Chords

The next family of seventh chords is the dominant seventh chords. Dominant seventh chords have a more tense sound than the major seventh chords. They are often used as a tension point to resolve to a more placid sound, or as stand-alone chords in a progression to offer a little more edge and bite to the sound.

The C dominant seventh chord is spelled C - E - G - B♭. It is a C Major triad with **the flat seventh scale degree added**. If you count from G to B♭, you find a distance of three half-steps or a minor third. This means that the dominant seventh chord follows the interval pattern of a **major third, followed by two minor thirds.**

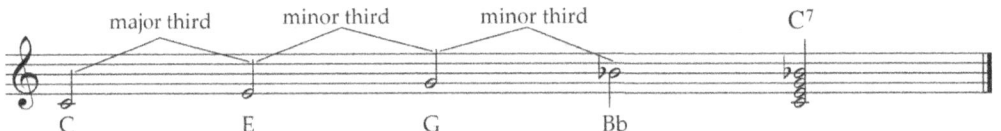

If we compare the notes of the C dominant seventh chord to the C Major seventh chord, we realize that the C dominant seventh chord has a lowered seventh degree, B♭ instead of B natural. This means the formula for any dominant seventh chord will be 1 - 3 - 5 - ♭7, or a major triad with a lowered seventh scale degree.

Here is a list of some common dominant seventh chords:

D dominant 7 : D - F♯ - A - C

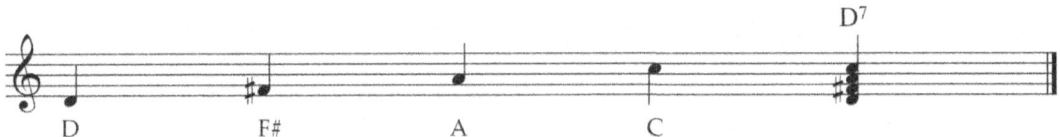

E dominant 7 : E - G♯ - B - D

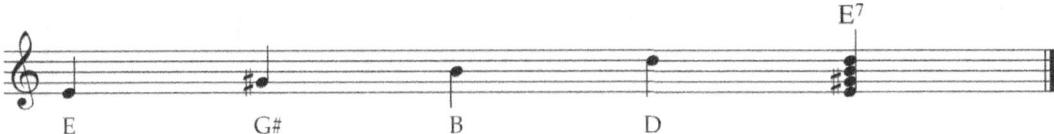

F dominant 7 : F - A - C - E♭

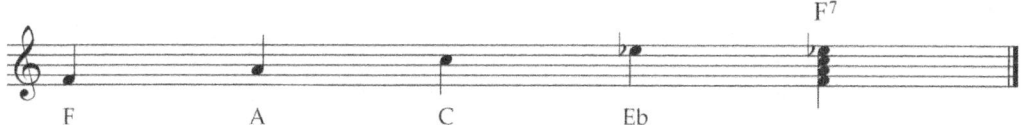

G dominant 7 : G - B - D - F

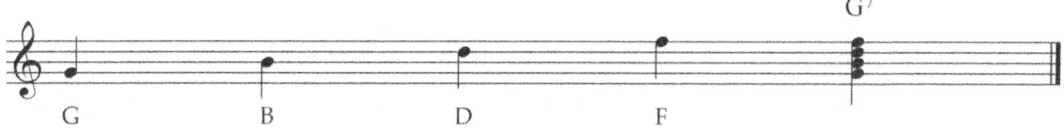

A dominant 7 : A - C♯ - E - G

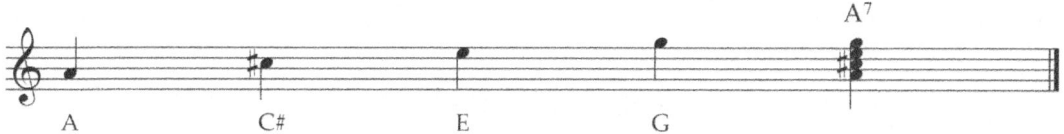

B dominant 7 : B - D♯ - F♯ - A

Minor Seventh Chords

Minor seventh chords are a smooth and pleasing tonality with a wide range of uses. You will hear minor seventh chords in jazz, blues, RnB, funk, soul, and more.

The minor seventh chord combines a minor triad with a flat seventh scale degree. Remember from Chapter 4, that a C minor triad is spelled C - E♭ - G. To turn this chord into a C minor seventh chord, we simply add the flat seventh scale degree, B♭, to the chord. This means a C minor seventh chord is spelled C - E♭ - G - B♭.

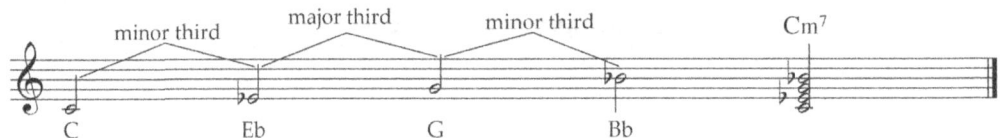

If we count from G to Bb, we find the distance of three half-steps or a minor third. This means that the interval structure of a minor seventh chord is a **minor third, followed by a major third, and then a minor third.**

If we compare the notes of a C minor seventh chord (C - Eb - G - Bb) to the notes of a C major seventh chord (C - E - G - B), we find that the C minor seventh chord has flat third and flat seventh scale degrees. This means the formula for any minor seventh chord is 1 - b3 - 5 - b7.

Here is a list of some common minor seventh chords:

D minor 7 : D - F - A - C

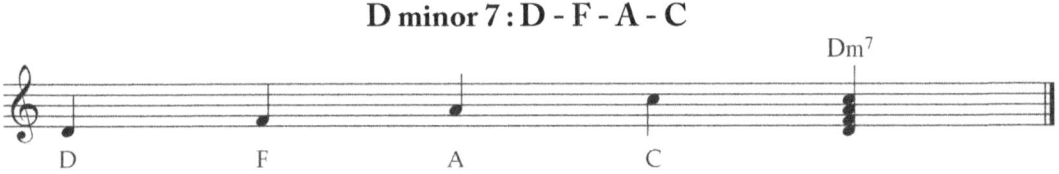

E minor 7 : E - G - B - D

F minor 7 : F - Ab - C - Eb

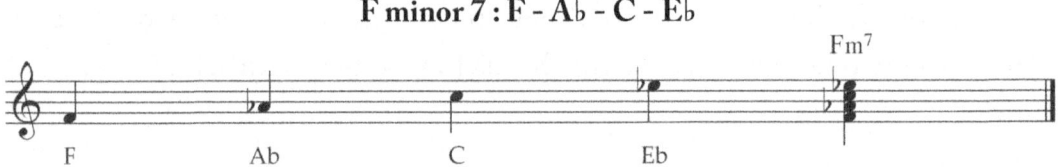

G minor 7 : G - Bb - D - F

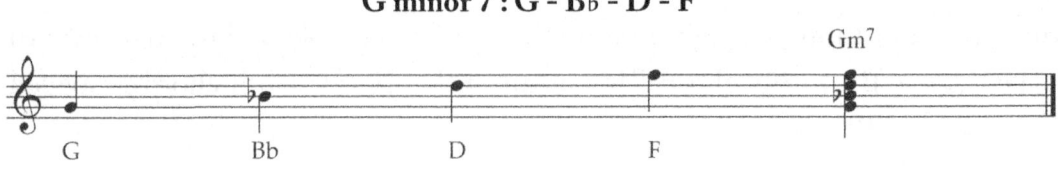

A minor 7 : A - C - E - G

B minor 7 : B - D - F♯ - A

Diminished Seventh Chords

The final family of seventh chords we will explore in this chapter are diminished seventh chords. There are two varieties of diminished seventh chords to explore: the **half-diminished** or **minor seventh flat five** chord, and the **fully diminished seventh** chord. Both varieties of diminished seventh chords are built on the diminished triad.

The half-diminished, or minor seventh flat five chord combines a diminished triad with an added flat seventh scale degree. The C minor seventh flat five chord is spelled C - E♭ - G♭ - B♭. If you count from G♭ to B♭, you will find a distance of four half-steps or a major third. This means the intervallic formula for a minor seventh flat five chord is **two minor thirds followed by a major third.**

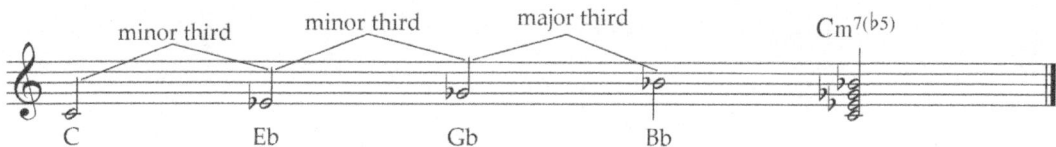

If we compare the notes of the C minor seventh flat five chord (C - E♭ - G♭ - B♭) to the notes of the C Major seventh chord (C - E - G - B), we find that the C minor seventh flat five chord has flat third, fifth, and seventh scale degrees.

This means the formula for any minor seventh flat five chord is 1 - ♭3 - ♭5 - ♭7. Here is a list of a few common minor seventh flat five chords:

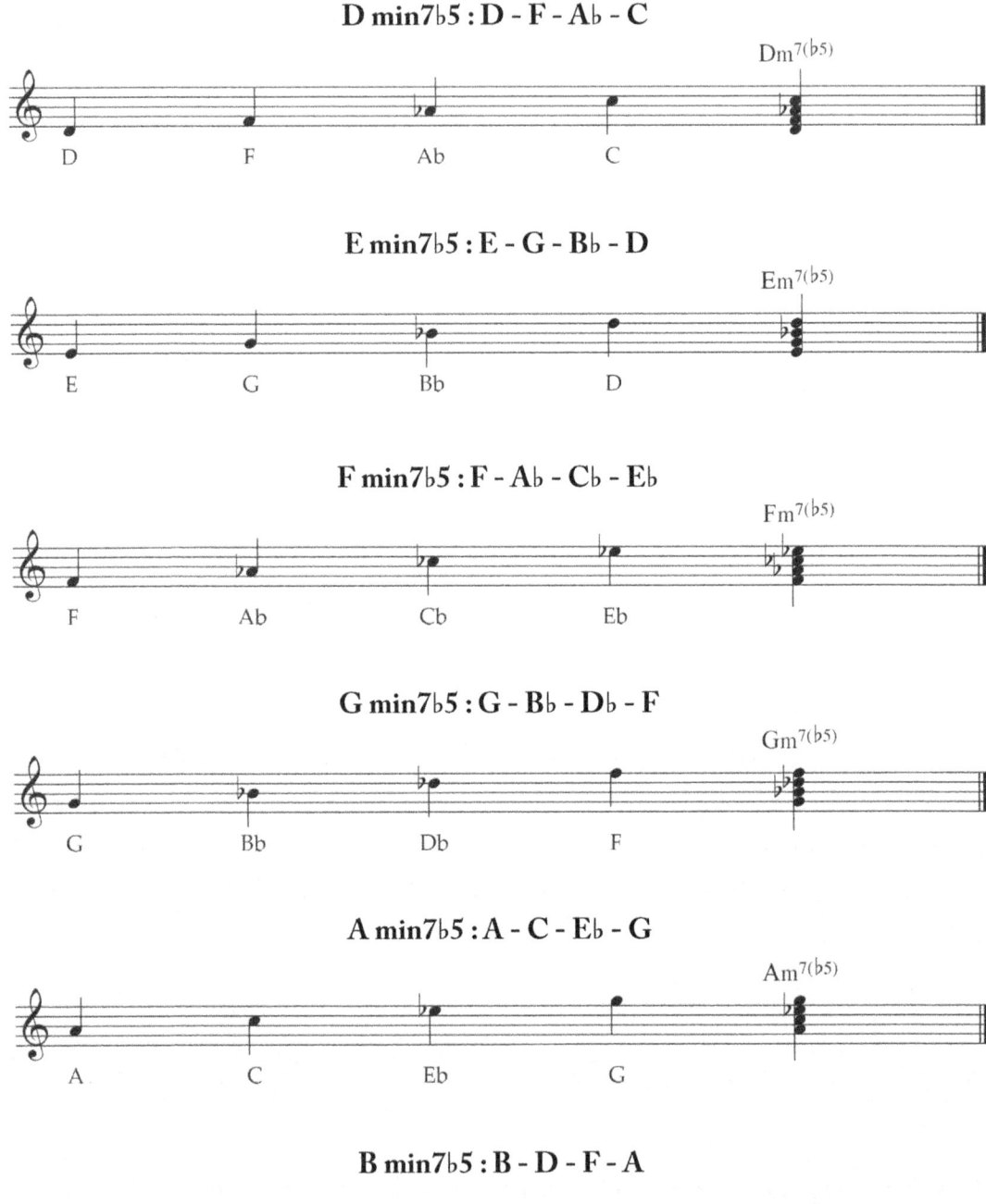

Exploring Seventh Chords

The fully diminished seventh chord takes the minor seventh flat five chord and lowers the seventh scale degree an additional half step. This means that the fully diminished seventh chord is composed of three minor thirds, making the chord fully symmetrical.

The C fully diminished seventh chord is spelled C - E♭ - G♭ - B♭♭. Yes, B double flat. Because the diminished seventh chord formula includes the seventh degree of the scale, we need to reflect this in our notation. So even though B♭♭ is the same note as A, we need to write B♭♭ in the chord to reflect the structure of the chord accurately.

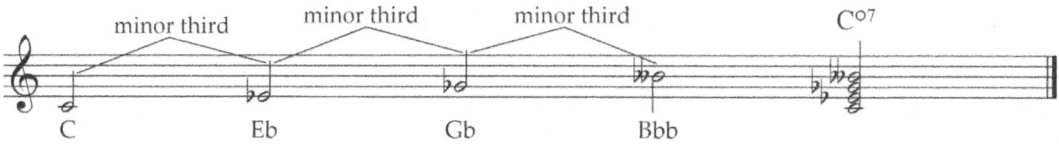

If we compare the notes of the C diminished seventh chord (C - E♭ - G♭ - B♭♭) to the notes of the C major seventh chord (C - E - G - B), we find the C diminished seventh chord has flat third, fifth, and double flat seventh scale degrees. This means the formula for any diminished seventh chord is 1 - ♭3 - ♭5 - ♭♭7.

Here is a list of some common fully diminished seventh chords. The superscript circle is a symbol used to mean a fully diminished seventh chord.

Building the Seventh Chord Scale

Now that we understand how seventh chords are constructed, let's see if we can apply this knowledge to the chord scale we developed for the major scale in Chapter 4 and build a chord scale of seventh chords.

We will use the following families of seventh chords to build this chord scale: major seventh, minor seventh, dominant seventh, and half-diminished seventh.

Remember that the pattern of triads in every major scale is major, minor, minor, major, major, minor and diminished. The chord scale for C Major looks like this:

Based on this information, what will the first seventh chord in our new chord scale be? If you said C Major seventh, you are correct! We can find this by continuing to stack thirds inside the C Major scale above the C Major triad. From C - E - G, we stack one more third above and find B. C - E - G - B spells C Major seventh.

Using the same method, can you figure out the second chord? Stacking an additional third above D minor makes D - F - A - C, or D minor seventh.

Stacking an additional third above E minor makes E - G - B - D, or E minor seventh.

Stacking an additional third above F Major makes F - A - C - E, or F Major seventh.

Stacking an additional third above G Major makes G - B - D - F, or G dominant seventh.

Stacking an additional third above A minor makes A - C - E - G, or A minor seventh.

Finally, stacking an additional third above B diminished makes B - D - F - A, or B minor seventh flat five.

All in all, this means the pattern of seventh chords in the major scale is:

Major seventh, Minor seventh, Minor seventh, Major seventh, Dominant seventh, Minor seventh, Minor seventh flat five

This is true for every single major scale. Check it out notated on the staff below:

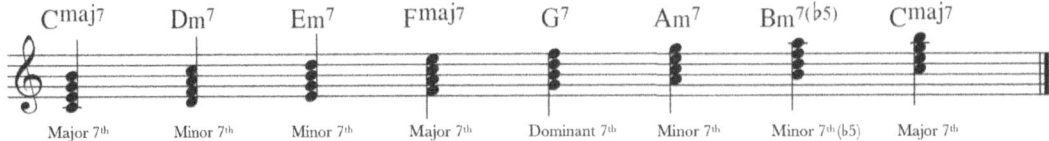

Chord Extensions

Beyond the realm of the seventh chords lies the expansive universe of **chord extensions**. Chord extensions are notes that are above the seventh scale degree. We can add these notes to our chords to increase their depth, density, and color.

So far, we have used stacking thirds to build our chords. We built the triad families by stacking major and minor thirds. Then, we stacked another third on top of the triad families to build the seventh chords. To access the extensions, we will continue with this concept.

When we travel above the octave, we will repeat notes one octave higher. That may seem obvious, but it is crucial to understand. We will continue to extend the scale degrees beyond seven, all the way up to fifteen.

For example, in the key of C, B is the 7th scale degree, C is the octave or 8th, and then we will call D the 9th, E the 10th, F the 11th, G the 12th, A the 13th, B the 14th, and C the 15th, or two octaves higher than our root.

If we notate this on the staff from middle C, it looks like this:

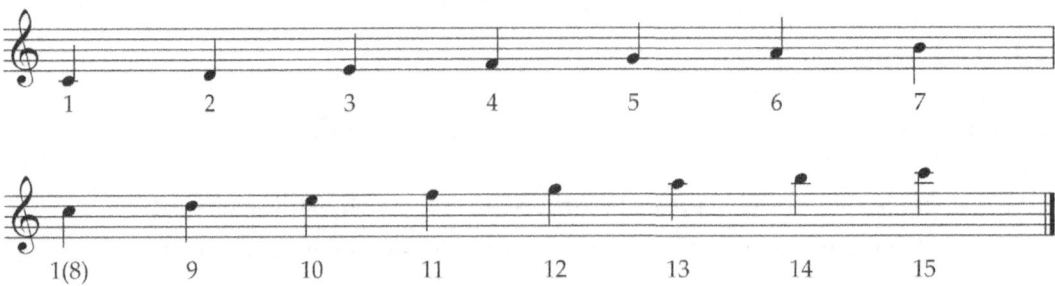

Now, if we continue to stack thirds above the 7th scale degree, it will look like this:

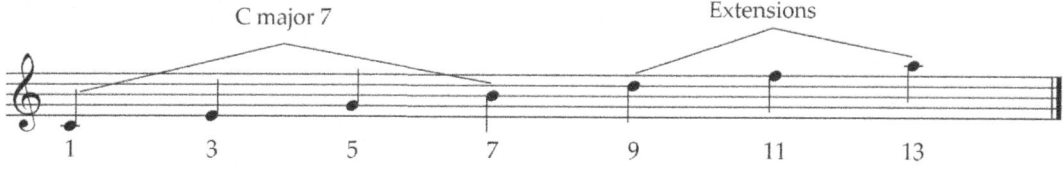

Stacking thirds shows that the most common extensions are the 9th, 11th, and 13th chord tones. You will hear these chord tones in jazz, classical, hip-hop, funk, and folk music. They add richness and depth to triads and seventh chords. Now we will check out a few examples of common seventh chords with extensions.

Major 9th

The major 9th chord is a lively and interesting texture. It is built by stacking an additional minor third on top of the major seventh chord. This means the interval structure for a major 9th chord is a major third, minor third, major third, minor third. The formula for this chord is 1 - 3 - 5 - 7 - 9. In the key of C Major the chord is spelled C - E - G - B - D. Check it out notated below:

Major 7th #11

The **major 7th #11** chord is an ethereal and otherworldly harmony that corresponds to the Lydian mode. The major 7th #11 adds a major third above the 9th scale degree. This means the interval structure for this chord is a major third, minor third, major third, minor third, major third. The formula for this chord is 1 - 3 - 5 - 7 - 9 - #11. In the key of C major, this chord is spelled C - E - G - B - D - F#. Check it out notated below:

Dominant 9th

The **dominant 9**th chord is one of the most useful chord extensions. It will instantly make your dominant chords sound more interesting. The dominant 9th chord includes an additional major third above the flat seventh degree, meaning that the intervallic structure is a major third, minor third, minor third, major third. The formula for the dominant 9th chord is 1 - 3 - 5 - b7 - 9. In the key of C major, this is spelled C - E - G - Bb - D. Check it out notated below:

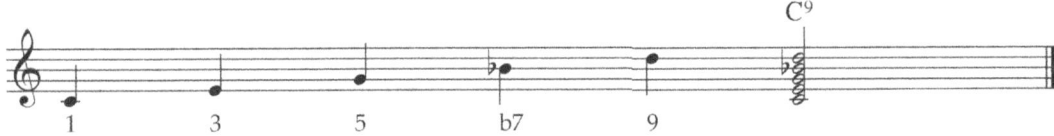

Dominant 13th

The **dominant 13**th is another extremely useful chord extension that will add color and depth to your dominant sounds. Often used in funk and soul music, the dominant 13th adds a minor third and major third above the flat seventh. This means the interval structure of the dominant 13th chord is major third, minor third, minor third, major third, minor third, major third. The formula for this chord is 1 - 3 - 5 - b7 - 9 - 11 - 13. Check it out notated below:

Minor 9th

The **minor 9th** chord is a dark and luscious harmony. To build this chord, add an additional major third on top of the flat seventh scale degree. This means the interval structure of a minor 9th chord is a minor third, major third, minor third, major third – the exact opposite of the major 9th chord. The formula for the minor 9th chord is 1 - b3 - 5 - b7 - 9. Check it out notated below:

Practice Time!

Use these questions and exercises to help practice your skills!

Chapter 8 Questions

1. What is a seventh chord? How many notes are in a seventh chord? What scale degree is added to the basic triad to create a seventh chord?

2. What are the four main families of seventh chords?

3. What is the interval pattern for a major seventh chord?

4. What is the interval pattern for a minor seventh chord?

5. What is the main difference between a minor seventh flat five chord and a fully diminished seventh chord?

6. What are chord extensions?

7. What are the most common chord extensions?

Chapter 8 Exercises

1. Practice building the following seventh chords:

2. Construct the following extended seventh chords by filling in the missing tones:

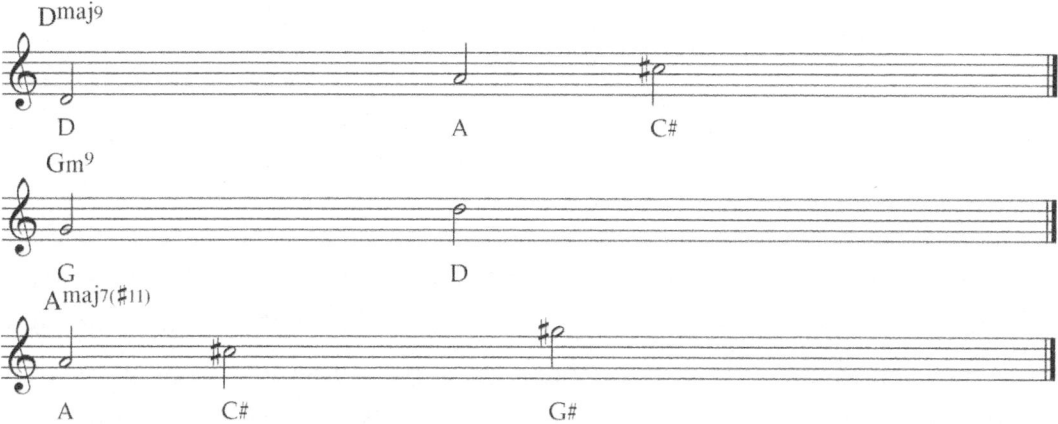

Conclusion

In Chapter 8, we broke open the world of harmony and explored the territory beyond the basic triads. The world of **seventh chords** is rich and offers many opportunities to expand your tonal palette and create interesting and beautiful sounds.

Many of your favorite musical artists and producers probably use **seventh chords** in their compositions, and understanding the basics of how seventh chords are built and used will be highly beneficial in your advancing knowledge of music theory. However, if you are having some difficulty grasping the concepts, revisit the material in Chapter 5 to make sure you have a strong understanding of triads and the practice of stacking thirds to build chords. This is foundational material.

In essence, seventh chords are four-note chords. Seventh chords are called such because they add some variation of the seventh scale degree to a triad. There are four main types of seventh chords: **major seventh, minor seventh, dominant seventh,** and two variations of diminished seventh chords (**half-diminished and fully diminished**). These chords are all built by stacking thirds above the triad.

Extensions are tones above the octave. When we continue the scale above the octave, we extend our scale degrees beyond eight all the way up to fifteen, or two octaves up. When we stack thirds, we realize the most common chord extensions are found on the 9th, 11th, and 13th scale degrees.

These extensions are also the most common because they add new tones to the chord. They are not redundant reiterations or doublings of tones already in the basic triad or seventh chord.

It takes time to absorb all this information. Do not be in a hurry. Take it slow, and make sure you practice and understand how these chords are built and what they sound like. It is extremely helpful to play these sounds on an instrument if you have one available, so you really understand what they sound like and how they are constructed.

9
Exploring Dynamics and Musical Markings

Keywords: Dynamics, piano, pianissimo, mezzo piano, forte, fortissimo, mezzo forte, crescendo, diminuendo, slur, metronome marking, tempo, ledger line, 8va, 8vb, segno, coda, Dal Segno, Da Capo

In Chapter 9, we will explore more music terminology, including how to describe volume, speed, and style. You will also learn some of the markings and symbols used in music notation for octaves, form and direction.

Dynamics: How Volume is Described in Music

Dynamics is the word musicians use to describe volume in music. Think to yourself for a moment about what words you would use to describe volume. Perhaps words like soft or loud or heavy or light come to mind.

Here are some of the symbols musicians use to describe volume:

pp   *p*   *mp*   *mf*   *f*   *ff*

Pianissimo (*pp*) means extremely soft and quiet. You will see this dynamic marking in sections of music that should be extremely delicate and light. Think of this dynamic like a whisper.

Piano *(p)* means soft or quiet. You will see this dynamic marking in sections of music that should be soft, but not as soft as pianissimo. Think of this dynamic like a quiet conversation you might have in an art museum or library.

Mezzo piano *(mp)* means medium soft. You will see this dynamic in sections that should be louder than *piano*, but not much louder. This dynamic is often used as a bridge to a louder or softer dynamic. Think of this dynamic like a calm conversation at breakfast or the distant sound of a bird early in the morning.

Mezzo forte *(mf)* means medium loud. This is a step above *mezzo piano*. You will see this dynamic in sections that should be louder than *mezzo piano*, but not yet fully loud. Like *mezzo piano*, this dynamic is often used as a pathway to other louder or softer dynamics. Think of this dynamic like a commercial plane flying far overhead or a normal conversation volume.

Forte *(f)* means loud or forceful. This dynamic is the opposite of *piano*. You will see this dynamic in loud sections of music, often a climactic point or other high emotion section. Think of this dynamic like a bustling train station, yelling, screaming, or an intense conversation, loud appliances, etc.

Fortissimo *(ff)* means very loud. This dynamic is the opposite of *pianissimo*. When you see this dynamic, you should be playing as loud and hard as you possibly can. Do not hold anything back. It's a no holds barred, full-throated, crank it to eleven type volume. Think of this dynamic as standing next to a train whistle or a jackhammer on your doorstep.

You will see dynamic markings notated below the notes they are referring to. Check out this diagram below for an example of dynamic markings in notated music:

Can you identify the dynamics in this passage?

The passage begins with *pianissimo* (very quiet), followed by *forte* (loud), and ends with *mezzo piano* (medium soft). Experiment with these dynamics on your own to get a feel for how you can use them in your creative music-making.

Linking Dynamics Together with Crescendo, Diminuendo, and the Slur

Did you notice in the previous example how the dynamics jump from one to another with no middle ground? This can be an effective strategy to elicit surprise, shock, or another emotional reaction. But what if you want a dynamic to change gradually over time?

Musicians use three tools to notate changing dynamics over time: ***crescendo***, ***diminuendo***, and the **slur**.

Crescendo

The ***crescendo*** symbol is used to notate increasingly louder dynamics. It looks like this:

The *crescendo* is used to notate a gradual increase in volume from a softer to louder dynamic. Usually, the length of the *crescendo* indicates the rate of increase in volume.

Here is an example of a fast *crescendo* in notated music:

Can you see how the *crescendo* has been used to indicate a gradual change in volume from *pianissimo* to *forte*?

Here is the same example with the *crescendo* extended. How do these two examples differ? What difference do the change in dynamics and the *crescendo* make? In the first example, the music gradually increases in volume to *forte* on the E-flat and then resolves into a medium soft (mezzo piano) on the A-flat. In the second example, the music increases in volume at a slower rate until reaching loud or forceful *(forte)* on the A-flat.

Diminuendo

A ***diminuendo***, sometimes called a ***decrescendo***, symbol is used to indicate a decrease in volume over time. It looks like this:

Diminuendo is the opposite of *crescendo*. Like the *crescendo*, the length of the *diminuendo* indicates the rate of decrease in volume.

Here is an example of a short *diminuendo*:

Here is an example of a longer *diminuendo*:

Here is the same musical example with both *crescendo* and *diminuendo* included:

In the latter example, we see music volume starting extremely soft *(pianissimo)*, gradually crescendo to loud *(forte)* on the E-flat and then gradually decreasing in volume down to moderately soft *(mezzo piano)* on the A-flat.

Slur, Legato Mark, or Phrase Mark

The last dynamic tool you will learn here is the **slur**, also known as the ***legato mark*** or the **phrase mark**. The slur is used to indicate the start, middle and end of a phrase of music. It is a more complex and nuanced way to notate music. The *legato* mark is not always included in written music but is a helpful tool in composing if you want to be extremely explicit about how you want something interpreted.

Check out the diagram below to see a slur in notated music:

This notation signifies that the phrase begins on F, reaches a high point on E♭, and concludes with A♭. It also tells you those notes should be played legato, which means smoothly with no gaps between the notes. The opposite of *legato* is **staccato**, where a note is slightly shortened so that a noticeable gap or silence is heard between the notes.

Employing the combination of *crescendo*, *diminuendo*, and a slur will make your music extremely clear and allow you to be as particular as you desire with your creation:

Beautiful, like a complete sentence or a fully formed thought!

Metronome Markings and Indications of Speed and Style

Let's take a moment to reflect on how you would notate the speed and style of a piece of music. What terms would you use? Where would you place these terms on the music?

The most common way to notate the speed of a piece is like this:

♩ =120

Music marking for Tempo

This means that the music is played at a speed of 120 quarter note beats per minute (bpm). The **metronome marking** is placed at the beginning of a piece of music, above the clef like this:

If the time signature is 4/4, the metronome marking will likely be based on the quarter note. If the time signature is 6/8, the metronome marking will likely be based on the eighth note.

There are a large number of terms that musicians use to describe speed and style. Some examples include:

Tempo: *Tempo* is a synonym for speed. If you want to sound like you know what you are talking about, use the word *tempo*.

Largo: Extremely slow and dignified in style. Generally, 40-60 beats per minute.

Adagio: Slowly, but not as slow as *largo*. Generally, 60-75 beats per minute.

Andante: A moderately slow *tempo*. Generally, 76-108 beats per minute. Walking speed.

Moderato: Moderate tempo. Generally, 108-120 beats per minute.

Allegro: Fast, quick, and bright. Generally, 120-168 beats per minute.

Presto, Prestissimo: Very fast, generally anything above 168 beats per minute.

Marking Octaves

Can you find middle C on the staff? What about the C one octave higher than middle C? What about the C two octaves higher than middle C? What about the C three octaves higher than middle C? Can you even write that C on the staff?

Yes, you can notate the C three octaves above middle C on the staff, but it is difficult to read with all of those **ledger lines**. Ledger lines are lines added to the staff to notate pitches that fall above or below the staff in the treble and bass clefs. But adding more lines take up lots of space, so musicians have a shortcut. Check out this symbol:

The expression "*8va*" is a musician's shorthand for "one octave higher." The diagram below shows it notated in music:

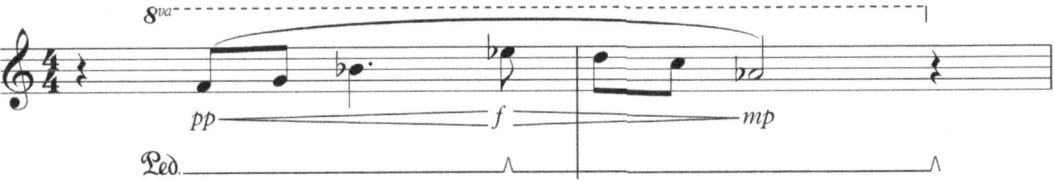

This notation means the passage is performed one octave higher than written.

To notate a shorthand "one octave lower," use this symbol:

8vb

Check out the diagram below to see this in notated music:

This notation means that the passage is performed one octave lower than written.

Marking Directives

Have you ever played a board game where one of the spaces made you jump back to the beginning or some earlier place on the board? You will encounter these types of directions in notated music as well. Think "playing" music, right?

There are four types of these directions in music notation that must be followed right after you see them:

Da Capo (D.C.) al Coda: return to the beginning of the piece, play up to the "*coda*" direction, and then jump to the next *coda* in the piece to continue.

Da Capo (D.C.) al Fine: return to the beginning of the piece and play up to the *fine*, which will be the end of the piece.

Dal Segno (D.S.) al Coda: return to the *segno* sign (see below), play up to the "to *coda*" direction, and jump to the *coda*, or ending, section of the piece.

Dal Segno (D.S) al Fine: return to the *segno* sign and play up to the *fine* or ending of the piece.

Symbol: Music Direction	
𝄋	= Segno (sign)
𝄌	= Coda (end)

Practice Time!

Use these questions and exercises to help practice your skills!

Chapter 9 Questions

1. What are dynamics? Why are dynamics important in music?

2. What is the musical word for an extremely soft dynamic? What about for a loud dynamic? Or a medium loud dynamic?

3. Does a *crescendo* mean an increase or decrease in volume?

4. What is the musical word for speed?

5. What is the musical word for "walking speed?"

6. What is the shorthand way to write one octave higher?

7. If you see *D.S. al Coda,* do you go back to the beginning or to the sign (*segno*)?

8. What is a *legato* mark?

Chapter 9 Exercises

1. Insert appropriate *crescendo* or *diminuendo* markings in this musical phrase:

2. Insert appropriate phrase or *legato* markings in this musical phrase:

3. Notate the following passage one octave lower using *8va*:

Conclusion

In Chapter 9, we took a brief tour through some common musical markings for volume, speed, and form. We learned about **dynamics** and the different markings musicians use to indicate volume. We learned about *tempo* and the different markings we can use to indicate the speed of music. We also learned a shorthand method musicians use to indicate where a passage should be played an octave higher or lower, and some formal markings to indicate repeated sections and endings. These are all useful tools that you will commonly see in notated music.

Practice using them and identifying them as you see them!

Final Words: Music Theory is the Key

By this stage, you have significantly increased your knowledge of the basic elements of music theory. You have learned the basics of musical notation, including how to read the treble and bass clefs, and how to build music with time signatures, rhythms, and rests. This is lifelong work that you will continue to practice and expand upon as you read more and more music.

You have learned how to measure and categorize intervals. You have also learned how to use these intervals to build scales and chords, and how to organize pitches with intervallic methods, such as the Circle of Fifths. This work will serve as a solid foundation as you move forward and begin to study and create the music that interests you.

At this point, you should begin to search out scores of the music you are curious about. Look at the chord progressions of rock, pop, and folk music. Try to analyze and understand the chord progressions and how they relate to the melodies.

If you are so inclined, take a look at the scores of classical music. You can learn a vast amount about harmony, scales, melody, and rhythm by investigating the history of classical music. From the chorales and fugues of J.S. Bach to the string quartets of Mozart and Beethoven, all the way to the serialism of Schoenberg or the minimalism of John Cage, you can spend a lifetime exploring the intricacies of music.

You can likewise use the tools you gained in this book to compose your own music. The most important steps in composing your own music are consistency and impartiality. Compose as often as possible, and do not be overly critical of what you are doing. If you do not like what you have composed, try something different. Get out of your own way and let the music flow. Above all, have fun exploring music theory!

Music has brought me daily joy for many decades, and I hope this for you too. This, and a lifetime of learning.

James Roscher
Author

Glossary of Keywords

8va: Shorthand marking for one octave higher.

8vb: Shorthand marking for one octave lower.

Aeolian: The Aeolian mode is the sixth mode of the major scale and is synonymous with the natural minor scale.

Augmented: In general, augmented refers to an interval or chord that has a fifth scale degree that is raised by one half step.

Bass clef: The bass clef is also known as the F clef because it tells us where F is on the staff. It is generally used to notate pitches below middle C.

Chord extensions: Chord extensions are notes added to chords beyond the seventh scale degree. The most commonly used extensions are 9ths, 11ths, and 13ths because these tones continue in the pattern of stacked thirds used to build chords (1 - 3 - 5 - 7 - 9 - 11 - 13).

Chord progression: A collection of chords moving in a sequence one after another.

Chord scale: The collection of chords built from the tones of a particular scale.

Chords: A chord occurs any time two or more notes are sounded simultaneously.

Circle of Fifths: The Circle of Fifths is a pattern of organizing all twelve tones a perfect fifth apart on a circle. The pattern displays the progression of key signatures or the sharps and flats that are added and subtracted to form particular keys. It is like a musical wheel and is a useful pattern to understand and reference when needed.

Coda: Musical term for the ending section of a piece of music.

Crescendo: Musical term for an increase in volume.

Da Capo: *Da Capo* means go back to the beginning. When paired with *al Fine* (*Da Capo al Fine* or *D.C. al Fine*), it means go back to the beginning and play to the *fine*, or ending. When paired with *al Coda* (*Da Capo al Coda* or *D.C. al Coda*), it means go back to the beginning and play to the *coda* section.

Dal Segno: *Dal Segno* means jump back to the *segno*, or sign. It is a tool used to mark repeated sections in a musical form. When paired with *al Fine* (Dal segno al Fine or D.S. al Fine), it means go back to the sign and play to the *fine*, or ending. When paired with *al Coda* (*Dal Segno al Coda* or *D.S. al Coda*), it means go back to the beginning and play to the *coda* section.

Diminished fifth: An interval of six half-steps.

Diminished triad: A three-note chord with the interval pattern minor third - minor third.

Diminished: In general, diminished refers to an interval or chord that has a fifth scale degree that is lowered by one half step.

Diminuendo: Musical term for a decrease in volume.

Dominant 13th: A dominant 13th chord is a dominant seventh chord with natural ninth, 11th, and 13th scale degrees added. The formula for the chord is 1 - 3 - 5 - ♭7 - 9 - 11 - 13. A C dominant 13th chord is spelled C - E - G - B♭ - D - F - A. However, some scale degrees are often omitted – you might only see C - E - G - B♭ - D - A for example. A dominant 13th chord is usually abbreviated as simply 13, as in C13 or G13.

Dominant 9th: A dominant ninth chord is a dominant seventh chord with a natural ninth degree added. The formula for the chord is 1 - 3 - 5 - ♭7 - 9. A C dominant 9th chord is spelled C - E - G - B♭ - D. You will often see the chord abbreviated as C9.

Dominant seventh: A dominant seventh chord is a major triad with a flat seventh scale degree added. It is a major triad with a minor third on top.

Dorian: The Dorian mode is the second mode of the major scale. It follows the interval pattern whole step - half step - whole step - whole step - whole step - half step - whole step. It is a minor scale with a raised sixth scale degree.

Dynamics: Musical terms for volume and expression.

Eighth note: An eighth note is a type of rhythm that receives ½ a count.

Eighth rest: An eighth rest is equal to ½ a count of silence.

Forte: Musical term for loud and strong. Abbreviated as **f**.

Fortissimo: Musical term for extremely loud and strong. Abbreviated as *ff*.

Fully diminished seventh: A fully diminished seventh chord is a diminished triad with a double flatted seventh scale degree. It is a diminished triad with a minor third on top. A fully diminished seventh chord is constructed entirely of minor third intervals.

Grand staff: The combination of treble and bass clefs connected with a bracket. Most piano music is notated on the grand staff.

Half note: A half note is a type of rhythm that receives two counts.

Half rest: A half rest is equal to two counts of silence.

Half step: A half-step is the distance from one pitch to the next highest or lowest pitch. From B to C is one half-step and E to F is one half-step. Half-step is synonymous with semitone.

Half-diminished/minor seventh flat five: A half-diminished or minor seventh flat five chord is a diminished triad with a flat seventh scale degree. It is a diminished triad with a major third on top.

Harmony: Harmony is a synonym for chord.

Harmonic minor scale: A scale like the natural minor scale, except that the seventh note is raised by a half-step.

Interval: An interval is the distance between any two pitches.

Ionian: The Ionian mode is the first mode of the major scale. It is identical to the major scale.

Key signature: The collection of sharps or flats inherent in a particular set of notes. In notated music, the key signature is found between the clef and the time signature.

Ledger line: Ledger lines are extra lines added above or below the staff to notate pitches that extend higher or lower.

Locrian: The Locrian mode is the seventh mode of the major scale. It follows the interval pattern half step - whole step - whole step - half step - whole step - whole step - whole step. It is a minor scale with lowered second, fifth, sixth, and seventh scale degrees.

Lydian: The Lydian mode is the fourth mode of the major scale. It follows the interval pattern whole step - whole step - whole step - half step - whole step - whole step - half step. It is a major scale with a raised fourth scale degree.

Major 7th ♯11: A major 7th ♯11 chord is a major seventh chord with a raised 11th scale degree. The formula for the chord is 1 - 3 - 5 - 7 - 9 - ♯11. A C major 7th ♯11 chord is spelled C - E - G - B - D - F♯. The ninth is not always represented in chord voicings however.

Major 9th: A major 9th is equal to 14 half-steps. In a scale, the ninth is the same note as the second, just one octave higher. A major 9th chord follows the formula 1 - 3 - 5 - 7 - 9.

Major scale: The major scale is a scale of seven notes with the interval pattern of whole step - whole step - half step - whole step - whole step - whole step - half step.

Major seventh: A major seventh chord is a major triad with the natural seventh scale degree added. It is a major triad with a major third on top.

Major third: An interval of four half-steps.

Major triad: A three-note chord with the interval pattern major third - minor third.

Major: Major refers to either a major third, as in the interval that defines a major triad, or a particular descriptor of a scale or an interval such as a major sixth, major second, or major seventh.

Measure: The basic building block of notated music. The top number of the time signature indicates how many counts are inside one measure. Measures are divided by vertical lines called measure lines or bar lines.

Melodic minor scale: A scale like the natural minor scale, except that both the sixth and seventh notes are raised.

Metronome marking: Musical marking used to indicate the number of beats per minute (BPM) in a piece of music.

Mezzo forte: Musical term for medium loud. Abbreviated as **mf**.

Mezzo piano: Musical term for medium quiet. Abbreviated as **mp**.

Middle C: The C note located in the middle of the grand staff, between the treble and bass clefs. The note is written one ledger line below the staff in the treble clef and one ledger line above the staff in the bass clef.

Minor 9th: A minor 9th refers to either the interval of 13 half-steps (C - D♭) or a minor 9th chord with the formula 1 - ♭3 - 5 - ♭7 - 9 as in C - E♭ - G - B♭ - D.

Minor seventh: A minor seventh chord is a minor triad with a flat seventh scale degree added. It is a minor triad with a minor third on top.

Minor third: An interval of three half-steps.

Minor triad: A three-note chord with the interval pattern minor third - major third.

Minor: Minor refers to either a minor third, as in the interval that defines a minor triad, or a particular descriptor of a scale or an interval such as a minor sixth, minor second, or minor seventh.

Mixolydian: The Mixolydian mode is the fifth mode of the major scale. It follows the interval pattern whole step - whole step - half step - whole step - whole step - half step - whole step. It is a major scale with a lowered seventh scale degree.

Modes: Scales that are derived from a parent scale that all share the same group of notes with a shifting root note or focal point.

Musical alphabet: In music, pitches are expressed as letter names in the musical alphabet. The musical alphabet is comprised of the following twelve letter names: **A - A♯ - B - C - C♯ - D - D♯ - E - F - F♯ - G - G♯**

Natural minor scale: A scale with the interval pattern whole step - half step - whole step - whole step - half step - whole step - whole step.

Notes: Another word that is commonly used in place of pitch is notes. Every note is a pitch. However, a note gives us a little more information beyond simply pitch, such as duration.

Octave: The octave is the distance from one note to the next highest or lowest note of the same letter name.

Perfect fifth: An interval of seven half-steps.

Perfect: Perfect is used to describe intervals of a fourth, fifth, unison, or octave. Perfect intervals are perfect because their frequency ratios produce whole numbers.

Phrygian: The Phrygian mode is the third mode of the major scale. It follows the interval pattern half step - whole step - whole step - whole step - half step - whole step - whole step. It is a minor scale with a lowered second scale degree.

Pianissimo: Musical term for extremely quiet. Abbreviated as **pp**.

Piano: Musical term for soft or quiet. Abbreviated as **p**.

Quarter note: A quarter note is a type of rhythm that receives one count.

Quarter rest: A quarter rest is equal to one count of silence.

Relative minor: The related minor key to any major key that shares all of the same tones. The relative minor of any major key is found on the sixth degree of the major scale.

Rhythm: In music, rhythm is the placement of sounds and silence in time. There are many different types of rhythms with different organizational methods.

Scale degrees: Scale degrees are a set of numerals assigned to each tone of a scale. Scale degrees are a valuable tool for exploring the hierarchy of pitches inside a scale or key.

Scales: A music scale is a set of notes within an octave arranged in sequential order according to pitch.

Segno: A musical symbol used to mark form, generally used to mark a repeated section.

Semitone: A semitone is the distance from one pitch to the next highest or lowest pitch. From B to C is one semitone and E to F is one semitone. Semitone is synonymous with half-step.

Seventh chords: Seventh chords are four-note chords. They are triads with an added seventh scale degree. There are four main families of seventh chords.

Slur: A slur, or *legato* marking or phrase mark, is a curved line used to indicate the start, high point, and end of a musical phrase. They are also used to indicate bowing directions in string music.

Solfege: *Solfege* is a syllabic system used to identify pitches inside a scale.

Staff: The series of five horizontal lines and four spaces that music is notated on.

Tempo: Musical term for speed.

Time signature: A time signature indicates how many beats are inside one measure and which type of note receives one count.

Treble clef: The treble clef tells us where the note G is on the staff. It is generally used to notate pitches above middle C.

Triads: A triad is a three-note chord.

Whole note: A whole note is a type of rhythm that receives four counts.

Whole rest: A whole rest is equal to four counts of silence.

Whole step: One whole step is two half-steps. From D to E is a whole step, as is G to A. A whole step is the same thing as a whole tone.

Whole tone: The whole tone is synonymous with the whole step. One whole tone is two semitones. From D to E is a whole tone, as is G to A. The whole tone is synonymous with the whole step.

ANSWERS: Question & Exercise

1. Exploring Pitch

Questions

1. The music alphabet is simply the collection of notes in our music system. There are twelve notes in the music alphabet. Written with sharps (♯), these are :

   A - A♯ - B - C - C♯ - D - D♯ - E - F - F♯ - G - G♯

It can also be written with flats (♭):

   A - B♭ - B - C - D♭ - D - E♭ - E - F - G♭ - G - A♭

2. One octave is the distance from one pitch to the next highest or lowest pitch of the same letter name. One octave is equal to twelve half-steps or semitones.

3. The staff is a collection of five lines and four spaces that we use to notate music.

4. The treble clef tells us where the pitch G is, specifically the G above middle C, also called G4. We recognize the lines of the treble clef using the mnemonic Every - Good - Boy - Does - Fine. We recognize the spaces of the treble clef with the mnemonic F - A - C - E or FACE.

5. The bass clef tells us where the pitch F is, specifically the F below middle C, also called F3.

6. The grand staff is the treble and bass clef combined and connected with a bracket. Piano music is commonly notated on the grand staff.

7. Middle C is called middle C because it is the C positioned in the middle of the grand staff. It can be notated one ledger line below the treble clef and one ledger line above the bass clef.

Exercises

1.

2.

3.

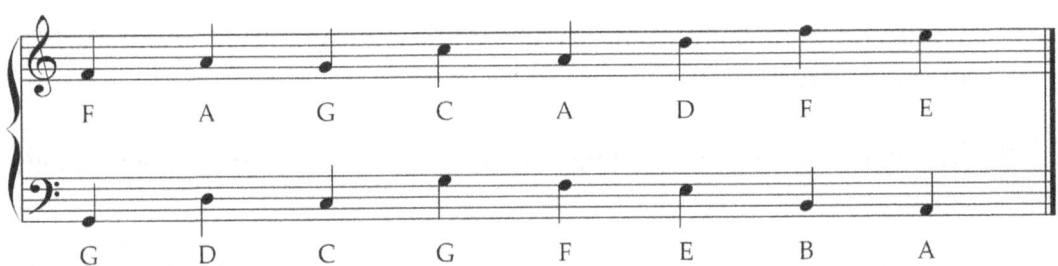

ANSWERS: Question & Exercise

4.

5.

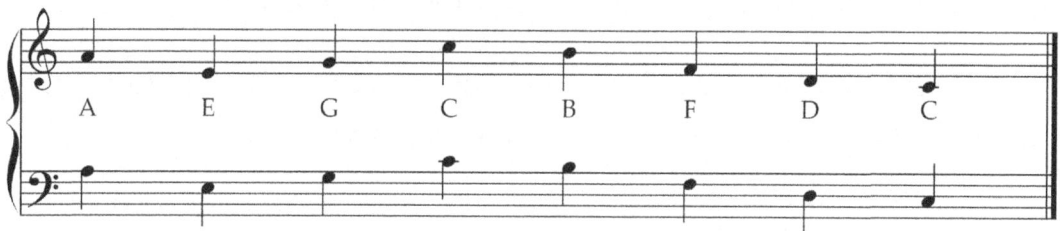

2. Exploring Rhythm

Questions

1. Rhythm is the placement of sounds and silence in time. The two essential tools used to organize rhythm are notes and rests, and time signatures.

2. The various notes are: whole note = 4 counts, half note = 2 counts, quarter note = 1 count, eighth note = ½ count, sixteenth note = ¼ count. Four (4) quarter notes equal a whole note, and two (2) eighth notes = 1 quarter note. A whole note lasts for four counts, a half note for two counts, and two eighth notes = 1 quarter note.

3. A dot next to a note adds half of the original value to the note length.

4. Rests are how silence is notated in music. The various rests are whole rest = 4 counts, half rest = 2 counts, quarter rest = 1 count, eighth rest = ½

count, sixteenth rest = ¼ count. A quarter rest = 1 count. There are four quarter rests for every whole rest.

5. A time signature is a tool for organizing rhythms into basic units called measures. The top number of the time signature tells us how many counts are inside each measure. All the rhythms inside the measure, which is divided by a vertical line called a bar line or measure line, must add up to the top number of the time signature. The bottom number tells us which type of note receives one count. Most commonly, time signatures have either a 4, meaning a quarter note receives one count, or an 8, meaning an eighth note receives one count, as the bottom number.

6. In a $\frac{4}{4}$ time signature, there are four beats in every measure. In a $\frac{6}{8}$ time signature, there are six beats in every measure.

Exercises

1. Dotted half note, whole note, quarter note, eighth note, dotted quarter note, sixteenth note, half note, dotted eighth note.

2. Half rest, quarter rest, whole rest, quarter rest, eighth rest, dotted quarter rest, sixteenth rest, half rest, dotted eighth rest.

3. One example:

ANSWERS: Question & Exercise

4. One example:

5. One example:

3. Exploring Intervals

Questions

1. An interval is the distance between any two pitches.

2. Intervals are measured in half-steps. Two half-steps equal one whole step. Another term for half-step (H) and whole step (W) are semitone and whole tone, respectively.

3. There are three half-steps in a minor third, seven half-steps in a perfect fifth, and ten half-steps in a minor seventh.

4. Melodic intervals appear sequentially with notes played one after the other, not simultaneously.

5. Harmonic intervals refer to notes played at the same time as in a chord. In a chord, notes are stacked on atop the other and played simultaneously.

Exercises

1.

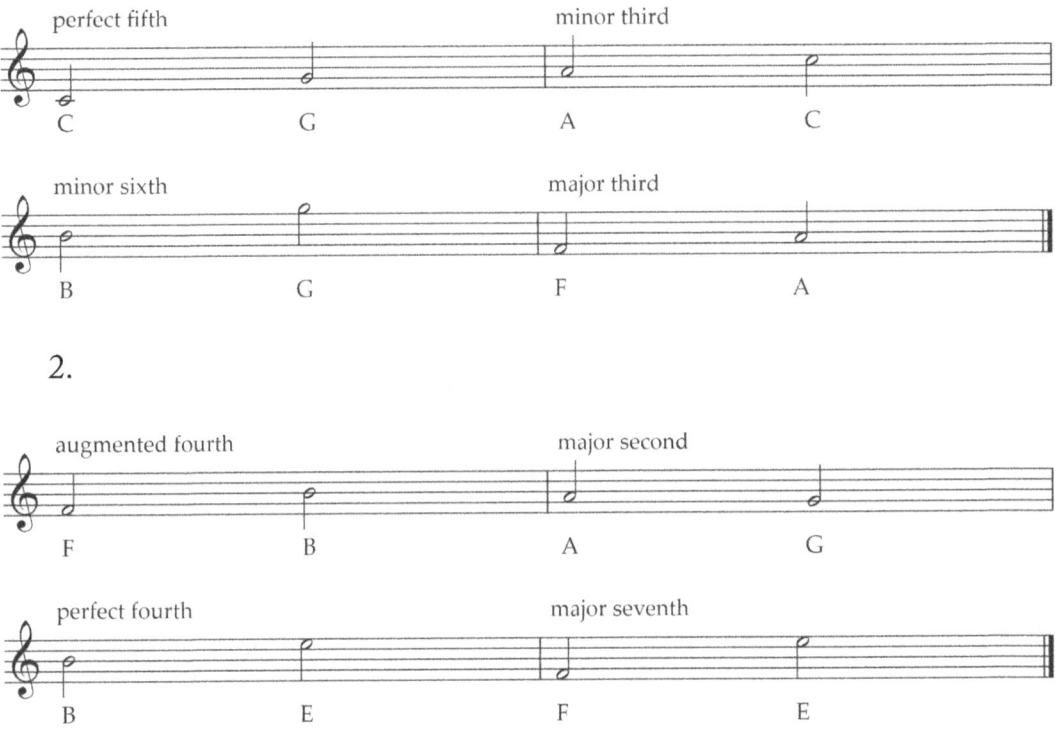

2.

4. Exploring Scales

Questions

1. A music scale is a set of notes within an octave arranged sequentially according to pitch.

2. The major scale is a musical scale that follows the interval pattern whole step, whole step, half-step, whole step, whole step, whole step, half-step (or, interchangeably, the whole tone and semitone terminology). The C Major scale is spelled C - D - E - F - G - A - B - C.

ANSWERS: Question & Exercise

3. The natural minor scale is a musical scale with the interval pattern whole step, half-step, whole step, whole step, half-step, whole step, whole step.

4. For every major scale, there is a relative minor scale that shares all the same pitches and vice versa.

5. Scale degrees are numerals assigned to every pitch of a scale. For example, in the C Major scale, C is 1, D is 2, E is 3, F is 4, etc. Scale degrees allow us to visualize the hierarchy of pitches in the scale, notice trends and directions in how pitches resolve to one another, and communicate information about scales and music.

6. The relative minor of any major key is found on the sixth scale degree of the major scale. The relative major of any minor key is found on the third scale degree of the minor scale.

7. The functional names of the scale are *tonic, supertonic, mediant, subdominant, dominant, submediant,* and *subtonic* or *leading tone*. The third scale degree is called the mediant, the sixth scale degree is called the submediant, and the scale's root (or the first scale degree) is called the tonic.

8. *Solfege* is a syllabic system that assigns a syllable to each pitch of the scale. It is a useful ear training tool. In the C Major scale, *do* corresponds with C and *sol* corresponds with G.

Exercises

1.

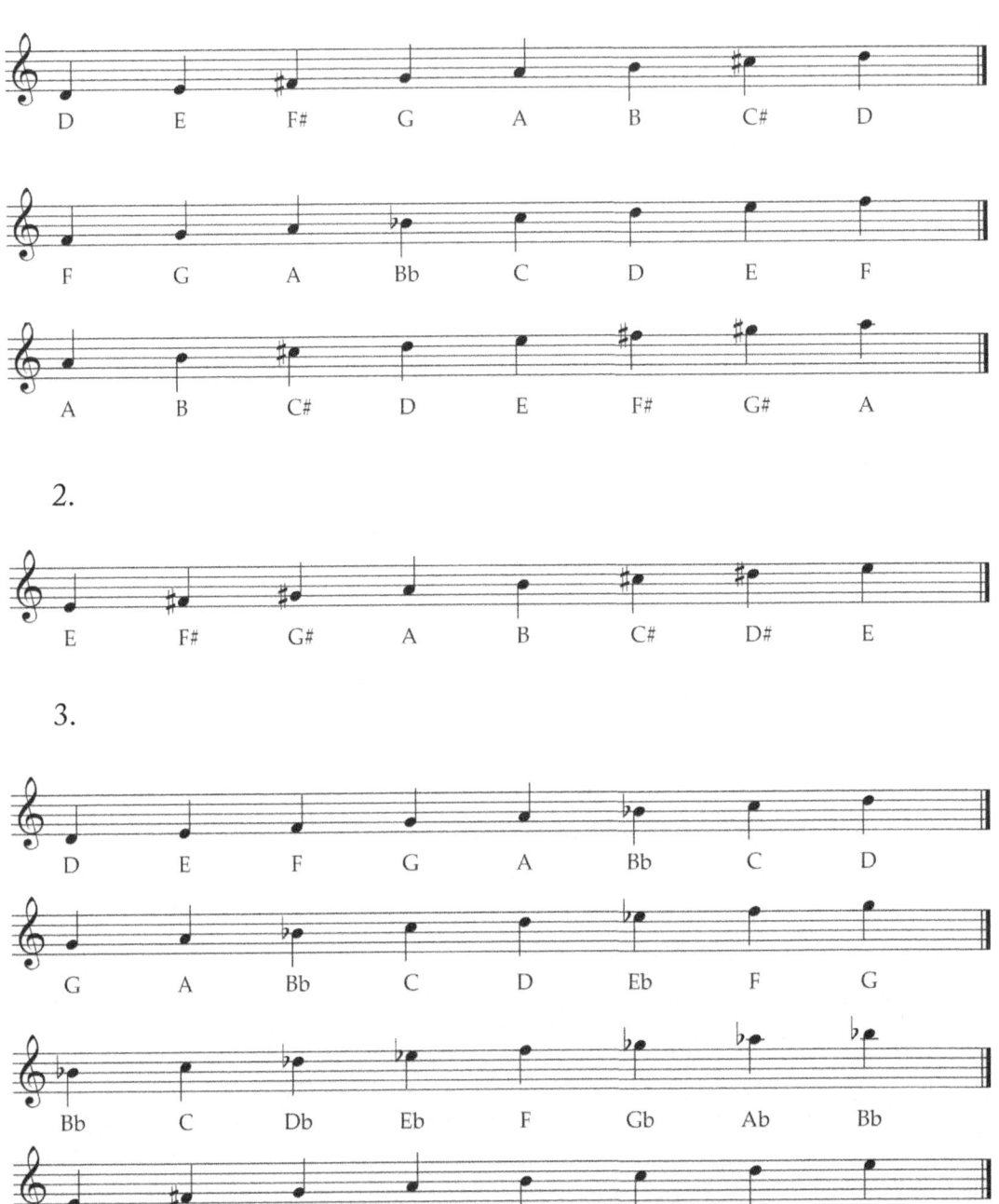

ANSWERS: Question & Exercise

4.

5. Exploring Harmony Through Building Chords

Questions

1. It only takes two notes to make a chord.

2. The most common type of chord is a triad. A triad has three notes.

3. The four main families of triads are: major, minor, diminished, and augmented.

4. The interval structure of a major triad is starting with the root, move up a major third and then a minor third. The interval structure of a minor triad is root, move up a minor third and then a major third. Major triads and minor triads have an inverse interval pattern.

5. A chord scale is the resulting harmonization of all the tones in a particular scale.

6. The Roman numerals are very similar to the scale degrees. Both tools show the function of the tone or chord in the scale. However, the Roman numerals can be upper or lowercase to distinguish whether a chord is major or minor.

Exercises

1.

2.

ANSWERS: Question & Exercise

3.

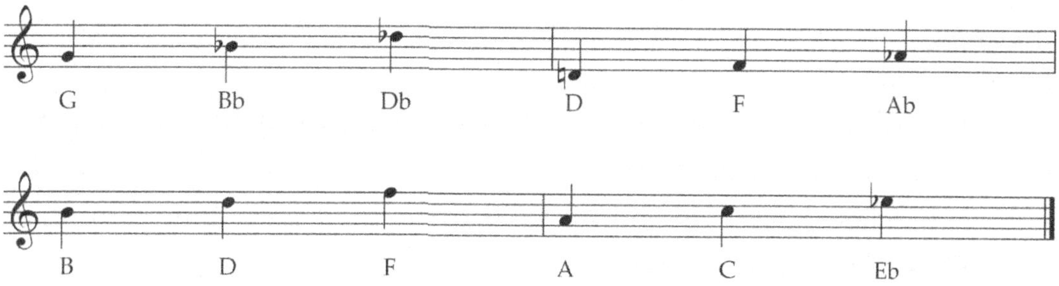

G   Bb   Db   D   F   Ab

B   D   F   A   C   Eb

4.

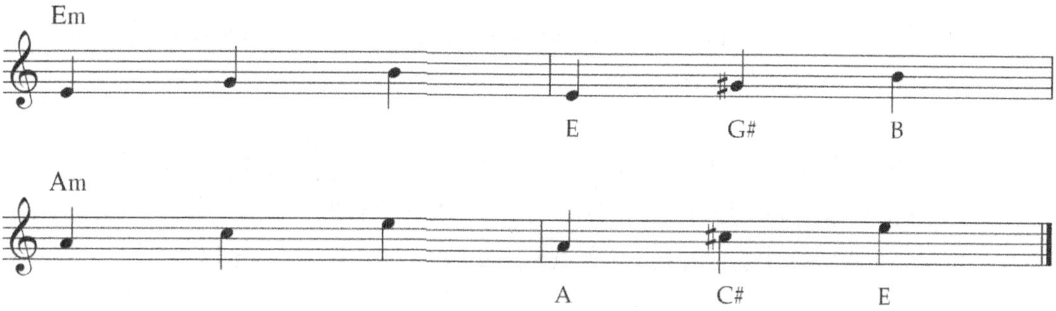

Em

E   G#   B

Am

A   C#   E

5. (a)

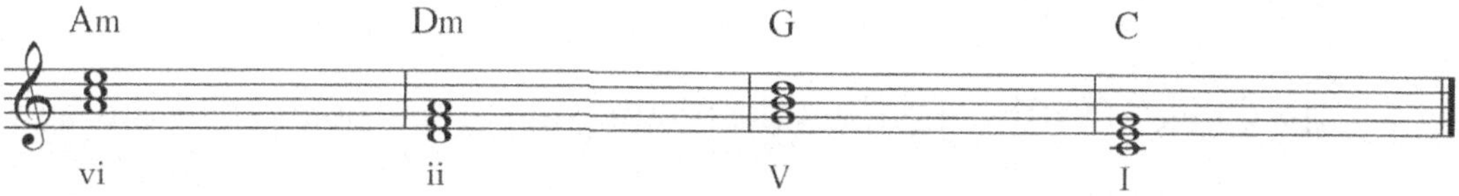

Am — vi
Dm — ii
G — V
C — I

(b)

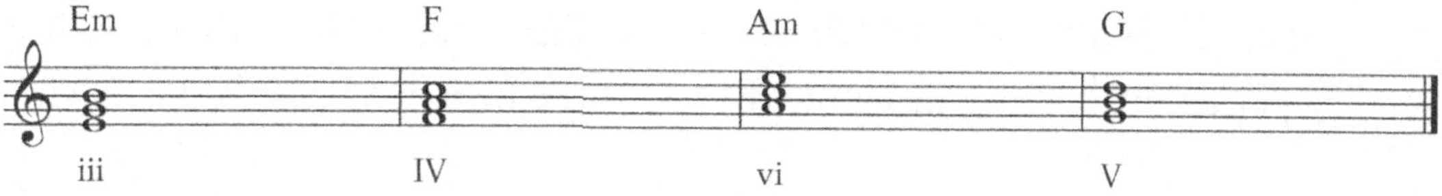

Em — iii
F — IV
Am — vi
G — V

(c)

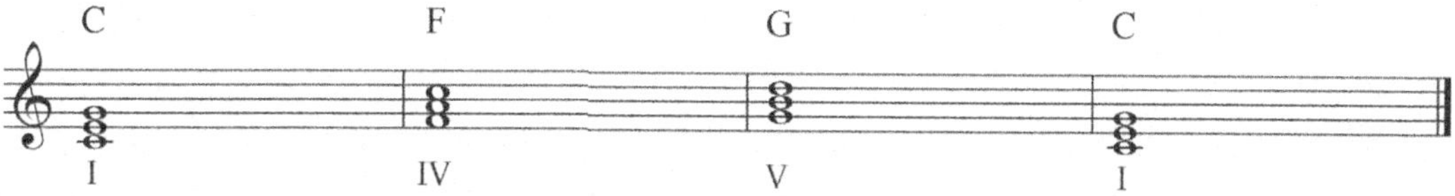

C — I
F — IV
G — V
C — I

6. Key Signatures & Circle of Fifths

Questions

1. A key is essentially a group of pitches organized in a hierarchical manner from a particular root note. The root note is always the name of the key. A key signature is shown as either sharps or flats right up front on the staff next to the cleft.

2. Generally, a key signature tells us what seven notes can be played for that piece of music and what chords are available to play as these will be built on the seven available notes. Key signatures will tell us if a piece has a major or minor key tonality.

3. The key of C Major has no sharps or flats, The keys with only sharps are G (1), D (2), A (3), E (4), B (5), F♯ (6) and C♯ (7). The keys with only flats are F (1), B♭ (2), E♭ (3), A♭ (4), D♭ (5), G♭ (6) and C♭ (7).

4. The Circle of Fifths is like a musical wheel. It is a way of organizing all twelve pitches, so they are each an equal distance of a perfect fifth away from one another.

5. The Circle of Fifths organizes the progression of sharps and flats through key signatures.

6. The progression of sharps and flats is mirrored in the progression of fifths around the Circle. Each new key adds a flat or sharp that is either a perfect fifth above or below the last sharp or flat.

Exercises

1.

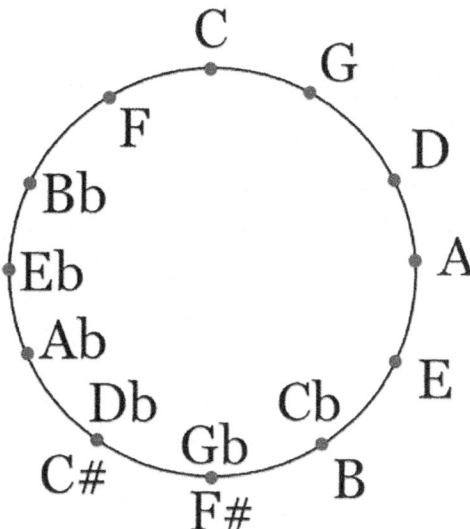

2. D major, E♭ major, B major, F major, D♭ major

7. Exploring the Modes

Questions

1. Modes are scales that are derived from a parent scale or set of notes. All modes in one key share the same basic set of pitches. The distinct characters of each mode are created by shifting the root or focal point of the mode.

2. There are seven modes: Ionian, Dorian, Phrygian, Lydian, Mixolydian, Aeolian, and Locrian.

3. The major modes include Ionian, Lydian, and Mixolydian. The minor modes include Dorian, Phrygian, Aeolian, and Locrian.

4. The defining feature of the Lydian mode is the raised fourth scale degree. The defining feature of the Dorian mode is the natural sixth scale degree. The defining feature of the Phrygian mode is the flat second scale degree.

5. Musical modes give you an expanded palette of emotional options beyond the standard major and minor dichotomy of happy or sad. Modes are so ubiquitous in contemporary music that it is essential to learn them. If you do not, you will lack a certain understanding and depth of knowledge about the possibilities of music. You will also miss out on understanding why certain music elicits a particular response.

Exercises

1.

8. Exploring Seventh Chords

Questions

1. A seventh chord is a four-note chord that is formed from various combinations of triads and a seventh scale degree.

2. The four main families of seventh chords are: major seventh, dominant seventh, minor seventh, and diminished seventh.

3. The interval pattern of a major seventh chord is major third, minor third, major third.

4. The interval pattern of a minor seventh chord is minor third, major third, minor third.

5. The main difference between a minor seventh flat five chord and a fully diminished seventh chord is in the seventh scale degree. A minor seventh flat five chord features a flat seventh scale degree (a major third above the fifth) while the fully diminished seventh chord features a double flat seventh scale degree (a minor third above the fifth).

6. Chord extensions are essentially notes that are above the seventh scale degree. We can add these notes to our chords to increase their depth, density, and color.

7. The most common chord extensions are found on the 9th, 11th, and 13th scale degrees.

Exercises

1.

2.

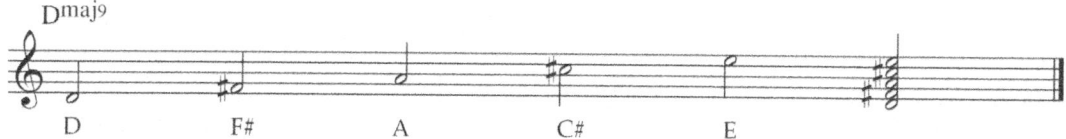

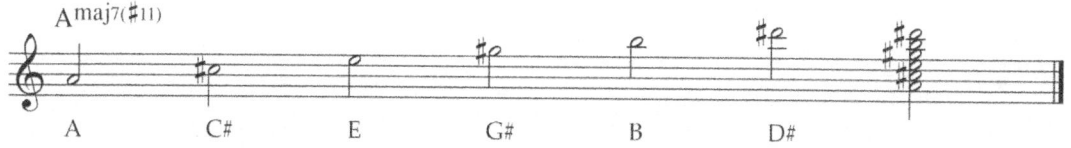

9. Exploring Dynamics & Musical Markings

Questions

1. Dynamics are words and markings musicians use to indicate volume, style, and expression.

2. The musical word for an extremely soft dynamic is *pianissimo*. The musical word for a loud dynamic is *forte*. The musical word for a medium loud dynamic is *mezzo-forte*.

3. *Crescendo* means an increase in volume.

4. The musical word for speed is *tempo*.

5. The musical word for "walking speed" is *andante*.

6. A shorthand method to notate one octave higher is *8va*.

7. If you see *D.S. al Coda*, you should go back to the sign or *segno*.

8. A *legato* mark, or a phrase marking or slur, is a curved line that indicates the start, high point, and end of a musical phrase. It differs from a tie in

that a tie connects two notes of the same pitch for an extended rhythmic value while a *legato* mark connects multiple pitches.

Exercises

1.

2.

3.

About the Author

James Roscher is a multi-instrumentalist and vocalist whose extensive experience in the field has made him a contemporary author of music books. With over 30 years of music knowledge, he weaves his expertise into his works, sharing thought-provoking insights on the power of music and its ability to bring people together.

About the Publisher

Musicora Publishing creates content to help aspiring individuals learn music theory simply and easily. Music theory is an essential component of any musician's education, but it can often be challenging for those new to the topic. Musicora Publishing makes learning music theory easy and fun, with content tailored specifically for modern learners. We believe anyone can learn music theory with the right tools and are committed to providing those tools to all who seek them. Join us on our mission to make music education accessible to everyone.

www.musicora.co

If you liked this book, please leave a review at www.amazon.com

We wish you persistence, discipline and success on your music journey.

Made in the USA
Middletown, DE
23 July 2024